For Peggy.
And for all the girls.
A reminder to always
strive for your dreams.

Publishing Director Sarah Lavelle
Editor Stacey Cleworth
Art Direction and Design Emily Lapworth
Cover and Illustrations Han Valentine
Photographers India Hobson
& Magnus Edmondson
Food Stylist Rob Allison
Prop Stylist Beck Hanson
Head of Production Stephen Lang
Production Controller Nikolaus Ginelli

First published in 2021 by Quadrille,
an imprint of Hardie Grant Publishing

Reprinted in 2021
10 9 8 7 6 5 4 3 2

Quadrille
52–54 Southwark Street
London SE1 1UN
quadrille.com

Cataloguing in Publication Data: a catalogue record
for this book is available from the British Library.

978 1 78713 776 9

Printed in China

PIPPA
MIDDLEHURST

BOWLS &
BROTHS

**Build a Bowl of Flavour from Scratch,
with Dumplings, Noodles and More**

PHOTOGRAPHY BY
INDIA HOBSON & MAGNUS EDMONDSON

Hardie Grant
QUADRILLE

CONTENTS

Introduction

I've always preferred eating from a bowl.

A large, deep bowl, the flavours of the ingredients already melded, ready and waiting to go. Uncomplicated eating.

At a table, in bed, curled up in an armchair, however I choose. A close second in the running for favourite flavour vessel is one that also provides one perfect mouthful after another – the sandwich. But that is a different book entirely.

The recipes in this book grew from a particular method that initially stemmed from fridge and freezer forages, or experiments in my home kitchen, usually while hungry. The findings of my forages, often humble ingredients, built and layered in such a way to create something sublime. And almost always sloshed into a large bowl.

I might find a simple chicken stock in the freezer, originally intended for wonton noodle soup. The jackpot! What a find! A simple stock has endless possibilities. I would begin by seasoning the bowl – adding the building blocks of flavour directly to the bowl I would eat out of.

Indulging my appreciation and enthusiasm for East and Southeast Asian flavours, I might choose some spicy, fermented *doubanjiang*, a little light soy sauce and black rice vinegar, a touch of sugar and some sour pickled mustard greens to add to the bowl. Pour in the hot stock to combine. Top with wheat noodles, a soft-boiled egg and a has-seen-better-days sliced spring onion (scallion). Or, whatever I had on hand.

Throughout these forages, building and layering from the bottom up, I found I was repeating the same pattern. As a molecular biologist by trade, repetition will always lead me to an efficient methodological process, from which a reliable formula appears.

This technique is not new, of course. Plenty of street-food vendors in East and Southeast Asia, from Taiwan to Thailand, cook this way. Endless individual bowls of sauce, seasoning, crunchy bits, fresh bits, herbs, aromatics, a starch, a protein – all neatly laid out on a street cart or stall and rapidly tossed into a bowl, with a lightning-fast flick of the wrist, landing in a melamine bowl in perfect, complementary amounts.

In Japan, for example, a flavourful tare sauce is added to the bowl prior to ramen broth, then noodles and toppings are added. All the ingredients brought together at the final moment, to maximize on their freshness, to layer and develop complexity of flavour.

As with this technique, the ingredients and combinations used in this book are inspired and informed by years of learning and experimenting with ingredients, techniques and flavours from across East and Southeast Asia, and powered by a deep love and respect. The areas of East and Southeast Asia represent a multitude of cultures and cuisines and the ingredients, skills and flavour combinations I draw upon here barely represent the tip of the iceberg. And while nothing can replace a lived experience, or growing up with home-cooked East and Southeast Asian food, I feel extremely lucky and happy to have been able to learn about these cuisines from a distance, researching and practising, over the years.

$\longrightarrow$

If you're interested in further reading, I'd thoroughly recommend *Silk Road Recipes: Parida's Uyghur Cookbook*, by Gulmira Propper, which explores the cuisine of the Uyghur people of Northwest China, and *Chicken and Rice: Fresh and Easy Southeast Asian Recipes From a London Kitchen* by Shu Han Lee. My favourite TV chef growing up was Ching-He Huang – I have all her cookbooks. Online, I am a big fan of The Woks of Life (@thewoksoflife), a family-run Chinese recipe blog – it's full of amazing recipes, including so much research. Red House Spice (@red. house.spice), a blog run by recipe developer and

photographer Wei, who also runs culinary tours of China and has become a friend, is a massive inspiration. And, I've learned so much from the recipes and writing of Grace Young (@stirfryguru), especially her book *The Wisdom of the Chinese Kitchen* .

The recipes I share here are largely non-traditional – happy accidents that made it into my regular repertoire, dishes created for supper clubs or homages to the classics adapted for my home kitchen. Regardless, they've all brought me comfort and satisfaction beyond measure and I hope they'll do the same for you.

Science of Broth

It's not necessary to know the ins and outs of the science behind a good broth to actually make a good broth – that's why we have recipes. But if your mind works anything like mine, then it certainly doesn't hamper the process.

Flavour is the entire experience – the taste, smell and texture of a food. Taste, on its own, is rarely satisfying without aroma. Texture's pleasure is fleeting and a great-smelling meal is a tease if you can't taste it, too. So, in learning to prepare a delicious bowl, full of perfect mouthfuls, we must learn to layer all these components and balance them to create harmonious flavour. Understanding this formula is key, and gives the tools needed to begin experimenting.

TASTE

Taste and smell are activated by different molecules and compounds, and these are all received differently by the receptors in our nose and mouth. Taste is received by the tongue, and salty, sweet, sour, bitter and savoury are delivered by molecules of sugar, salt, sour acids, amino acids and alkaloids. Interestingly, some sensations are not in fact tastes at all – the heat we feel from chillies, for example, is actually received by pain receptors, but we perceive this as a form of taste.

Furthermore, our tongues and mouths experience protein, fat and carbohydrates differently, and compounds are received by our receptors in different ways, depending on how they're travelling. Because fats hold onto aroma molecules, they transport them better. So if the flavour of roasted garlic and Sichuan pepper travels into your mouth riding on the back of a chicken fat molecule – a fat molecule being the safest and most reliable form of transport for a flavour molecule – it's not only going to *taste* different than if it entered your mouth in a liquid, but it's going *feel* different (read: *better*), and so we can use this knowledge to help build complexity of flavour. To create layers of flavour, we need liquid *and* fat to deliver taste, aroma *and* mouthfeel to achieve balance.

TEXTURE

Texture is incredibly important. Crunch is received by the mouth, the lips and also the ears. The resistance we feel when crunching into something crispy contrasts with softer things within a dish. Soft and melting textures, such as slow-braised meats, feel buttery and satisfying. Firm and springy textures that require mechanical intervention (chewing) provide interest. Textures also change when they're next to a different texture. Noodles sat in broth will absorb liquid and soften over time. Crunchy toppings added to a wet dish will absorb moisture and become soggy. Sometimes, the effect of osmosis is desirable, and sometimes it's not.

If we split tastes and textures into top notes or bass notes – I used to play first violin in an orchestra – we see the necessity for all the sections to play together, in sync, to make the final symphony. Too much bass, and the piece is darkened and overshadowed, with offbeat percussion the whole piece is thrown off balance, an out of tune woodwind melody and that's all you can hear. I see building and layering flavour in the same way – the end goal is well-rounded, nuanced and harmonious. When I'm building a dish, I think to myself 'what note does this ingredient play?'.

SMELL

Smell can cause remarkable psychological and physiological responses, more so than other senses as the aroma receptors in our nose (our olfactory receptors) have a direct connection to our amygdala, the part of our brain responsible for memory and physiological responses. We evolved this way because smelling something is a preliminary way to examine a food, in addition to sight.

Aroma helps us to distinguish between toxic and nontoxic foods – it's a safety mechanism. Ever recoiled from the smell of the bin? That's our body reacting to protect us from consuming potentially harmful substances. So it makes sense that when we smell a food or a dish that is full of flavour, we feel that comforting excitement, the deep-inhale-close-your-eyes-and-scrunch-your-shoulders feeling. This is our body telling us 'this is good, this is nutritious, this contains calories and energy, it will help your body survive, eat it'. Our salivary glands begin to produce saliva as our digestive tract kicks into action way before we've even put anything into our mouth.

These physiological and psychological responses then get hardwired into our brains. Neural pathways form to ensure we receive this exact same response when we detect that smell again. Of course, this mechanism is less about safety nowadays, but nevertheless it remains and serves a different purpose. Smell helps us remember and can even change our mood. This contributes to our emotional connection to food and the overall experience of flavour.

HEAT & TIME

The effect of resting broth overnight is another crucial piece of knowledge – yes, your takeaway curry did taste better the next day. When you're making a dish, and you want to eat it now (I've been there), I think it's useful to know what's happening on a molecular level, so you can make a truly informed (and obviously massively important) decision about when to use your broth – now, or tomorrow?

When heated, aromatic ingredients within food are subjected to many chemical reactions producing specific aroma and taste compounds. These reactions begin to cease when the broth is removed from the heat source. When you taste a freshly made broth, you experience each aroma compound individually, fresh off the back of a chemical reaction. This means stronger, more pronounced aromas will come to the fore and others, such as glutamate, will disappear in the background. Complex carbohydrates break down into simpler sugars, which taste sweeter. Proteins break down further releasing glutamate and other flavourful amino acids from their protein structure that enhance flavour. After resting, these compounds meld and mix and are more readily available to our taste buds, and so are received as one harmonious flavour, rather than one or two more pronounced flavours fresh out of a reaction. Essentially, all our hard work in balancing the broth correctly cannot truly be appreciated until the dish has cooled and rested.

Our broth represents the base of the dish, the backbone. After a broth has rested, we can then further layer and add new and fresh tastes and textures. Some might have been maturing on their own – chilli oil, for example. We might add ramen noodles for bounce and body. Something crunchy (crispy shallots), something soft and melting (meat perhaps), a sprinkle of something nutty (toasted sesame seeds?), the fresh zing of herbs (coriander/cilantro) or alliums (spring onion/scallions) or citrus (lime juice). A layer of fat (as we know), too, is super-important for mouthfeel and aroma.

By layering ingredients in this way, top notes and bass notes combine, and our finished dish sings. This is how we build complexity. We can create new flavours that go beyond the taste of the original ingredients and that, to me, is magic.

Getting Started

Equipment

A GOOD BOWL

From my experience, the number-one piece of advice is to invest in a good bowl. My favourite is around 18cm (7in) wide and 8cm (3¼in) deep – you need a bowl that is wide and deep enough to allow for movement so the ingredients can mix and meld together. You can find noodle and ramen bowls in Chinese or other Asian supermarkets or invest in a piece from your favourite ceramicist.

NON-STICK FRYING PAN (SKILLET)

My second piece of advice is to invest in a good non-stick pan and hide it from everybody else who uses your kitchen! A good non-stick pan will give you the best results when frying dumplings or trying to achieve a crispy skirt on fried eggs. (And trust me, that skirt is non-negotiable.)

MEASURING SPOONS

When seasoning individual portions, it's really important to use the correct amount as over- or under-seasoning will easily occur when using such small amounts. Everyday dessert, soup and teaspoons vary massively in their volume and cannot be used reliably to measure ingredients.

DIGITAL SCALES

When it comes to making noodles, especially, precision is key and I use digital bakery scales set to two decimal places, but these can be expensive. Salter is an affordable alternative.

PASTA MACHINE

Once you've made your noodle dough, you'll need to work it and shape it – and that's where a good pasta machine will more than earn its place in your kitchen. I have the Marcato Atlas 150 and it comes with various attachments for different shapes and widths of noodle.

RICE COOKER

For me, a rice cooker is essential in achieving consistently fluffy, individual grains of rice although I have a recipe which uses both a rice cooker and saucepan on page 157.

STOCKPOT

We'll be making a lot of broths and stocks in this book and a large 5L (175fl oz) stockpot is what I use throughout.

Preparation

MEASUREMENTS

The dough recipes within this book were made and tested using metric measurements. I would always suggest using scales to weigh out your ingredients for accuracy and peace of mind.

USE YOUR FREEZER

When used to its full potential, the freezer can be the source of all the ingredients needed to rustle up a delicious bowl of noodles or dumplings at various stages. When making broth, bones, carcasses and chicken feet can all be thrown into the pot straight from the freezer. A lot of butchers will give chicken carcasses and beef bones free of charge, and these can be stored in the freezer until needed. When using tiger or king prawns (jumbo shrimp), I save the heads and shells in a bag in the freezer, ready to use in shellfish stock. A finished broth can be portioned into freezer bags – simply pop the icy block of broth into the pan and heat. Dumplings freeze really well when laid on a baking sheet lined with baking paper – once frozen solid, transfer to a freezer bag to take up less room. They too can be cooked straight from frozen.

CLEANING BONES

Blanching and cleaning bones prior to using them in a broth is a golden rule. I've learned that this is a technique that has been used in East and Southeast Asian cooking for generations to remove impurities. Skipping the blanching can affect the overall flavour of the broth, and will cloud the broth. The easiest way is to dump the bones into the largest pot you own. Cover with cold water and bring to a rapid boil for 5 minutes. Impurities will rise to the surface. Pour the bones into a large colander and discard the water. Clean the pan and run the bones under cold water. Scrub with your fingers to remove any dried blood, grit or dirt. Once cleaned, return to the pot, add fresh water and let the broth-making commence.

STARTING A BROTH FROM COLD

Always begin a broth with the blanched bones and aromatics in cold water. A slow and gradual increase in temperature allows water-soluble proteins to escape and clump together, and this forms scum on the surface that you can remove by skimming the surface with a spoon. Adding ingredients to a boiling pot will cause proteins to remain separate and suspended in the broth, impairing the flavour and causing it to be clouded. The exception to this rule is when making *tonkotsu* or *paitan* broths – here, we need a rolling boil and the desired result is a cloudy, thick and creamy broth, created from emulsified proteins and fats.

STRAINING BROTH

The broths in this book will require straining at some stage in the cooking process. This can be done by straining the whole lot and decanting the finished broth into containers for the fridge or freezer. Strain through a fine mesh sieve (strainer) lined with muslin (cheesecloth) to ensure any small debris is removed, leaving you with a silky smooth and clear finished broth.

GRATING AND GRINDING

To get the best out of aromatic ingredients such as garlic, ginger and *galangal*, always use force. The aromatic oils and flavour (aroma and taste) compounds of these ingredients are housed within plant cells, which have cell walls. To get the flavour out, we need to break these walls. Cutting with a knife, or the blade in a food processor, merely separates the plant cells from one another, but the flavour remains inside. When we use a grater or a pestle and mortar, this applies force to the cell wall, causing it to rupture and open, releasing the flavour compounds. When adding ginger to a broth, I will give it a quick bash with the flat side of a knife, to bruise it and break those cell walls. When adding herbs at the end of a dish, tearing, rather than cutting, will impart more of their flavour. Even if a recipe calls for chopped garlic, I always grate it.

Ingredients

See page 176 for a list of online suppliers.

CHICKEN FEET

I have found that using chicken feet is a great way to add body to broths and give a beautiful silky mouthfeel. You can find them in Chinese supermarkets in the freezer section. Throw them straight into the pot from the freezer. They have a large surface area and are made of connective tissue, fat and bone – the good stuff. If you can't find chicken feet, chicken wings will also do the trick.

CHICKEN STOCK POWDER

In my kitchen, Amoy chicken powder is an indispensable ingredient. Utilized widely across East and Southeast Asia as a seasoning to add salt, MSG and a combination of herbs – it's the ultimate savoury seasoning.

CHINESE SESAME PASTE

Chinese sesame paste is made from toasted sesame seeds – unlike most Middle Eastern tahini, which is made from raw sesame seeds – and so has a uniquely rich and nutty flavour. Wangzhihe has become my favourite brand.

CHINKIANG BLACK RICE VINEGAR

Chinese black vinegar, also known as *Chinkiang* vinegar or *Zhenjiang* vinegar originates in the city of Zhenjiang, in the eastern coastal province of Jiangsu, north of Shanghai. It is made from fermented black rice and provides a super-mellow and slightly sweet acidity. It's great in dips or dressings. Once opened, store in a dark cupboard with the lid tightly screwed on – this vinegar can lose its zing if sat around for a while.

CRISPY FRIED GARLIC

You could of course make your own fried garlic, but any time I call for crispy fried garlic in these pages, I'm talking about the store-bought stuff.

DASHI POWDER

Dashi is a Japanese broth made from dried kelp and dried smoked tuna and you'll see it in everything from ramen, to sauces and marinades. Dashi is easy enough to make yourself but for dishes when just a splash is needed, I opt for dashi powder, which you dissolve in boiling water.

DRIED SHIITAKE MUSHROOMS

Dried shiitake mushrooms are a great store-cupboard ingredient. They can be rehydrated and used in stir fries or dumplings, with the soaking liquor providing an umami punch to broths or sauces.

EGGS

Whether used in noodle dough, as marinated ramen eggs, or for the desserts, I prefer to use organic eggs.

FISH SAUCE

Fish sauce is made from salted and fermented small fish, often anchovies. It adds salt, umami and depth. Like soy sauce, it can be fermented for anything from months to years.

FROZEN SEAFOOD

I always found it incredibly difficult to find good-quality seafood without venturing to the fishmongers. That is, until I found the frozen seafood section of my local Chinese supermarket. The quality and price is unmatched and I find all the variations I could wish for – shell-on, head-on, head-off, deveined, cleaned, portioned – whatever level of preparation you need. I always buy head-on/shell-on tiger or king prawns (jumbo shrimp) and freeze the head and shells for stock.

FURIKAKE

This Japanese seasoning is typically used over rice and is an umami powerhouse, usually containing sesame seeds, dried seaweed, and sometimes dried fish.

HIGH-PROTEIN FLOUR

The noodle recipes in this book call for high-protein flour. You can find the protein level of a flour by checking the nutritional information on the packet. Usually, this is given as grams per 100g. A protein level of 11–12% is classed as high and is perfect for making dumplings and noodles (higher than 12% would be found in a strong bread flour, for example). The higher the level of protein, the higher the level of gluten will eventually develop within the dough. A strong gluten structure is important for good texture in a noodle. This is especially important for hand-pulled noodles, where a strong gluten structure is integral to the pulling process. You can read more about the science of noodles in my first cookbook, *Dumplings and Noodles*. I use Blue Twin Spoons high-protein flour in all of my recipes.

KANSUI

When heated, sodium bicarbonate ($NaHCO_3$) undergoes a decomposition reaction, forming sodium carbonate (Na_2CO_3) water and carbon dioxide (CO_2). This increases its pH from around 8 to over 11, making it an alkali salt, otherwise known as *kansui*. In commercial ramen production, a combination of alkali salts are used depending on the properties required from the noodle, i.e. thick, thin, hard or soft. Potassium carbonate (K_2CO_3) is also sometimes used in combination with sodium carbonate.

When an alkali is added to noodle dough, it changes the bonding properties of the gluten strands. The alkali conditions increase bond formation between the strands of gluten, making the network tighter and firmer. This leads to a chewier and springier noodle that will absorb water less quickly, which is perfect if the noodle is destined to be sat in a bath of hot soup. You can buy it online, or as a liquid also known as lye water, but you can also make it easily at home.

Bake 100g (3½oz) bicarbonate of soda (baking soda) on a foil-lined tray at 120°C/100°F fan/250°F/gas mark ½ for 1 hour. The powder will lose about one quarter of its weight. Remove the kansui from the oven and transfer to an airtight jar by lifting the foil, creating a crease, then pouring it in (taking care to avoid contact with your skin as you do). Do not let the kansui come into contact with the open air for too long or it will absorb moisture and become less effective. It will keep sealed for up to one month.

KOMBU

Kombu powder, also known as powdered kombu dashi, is a dried, ground seaweed and my favourite way to replace salted fish ingredients, such as fish sauce or *katsuobushi* flakes, in vegan recipes, such as my ultimate vegan ramen (page 82).

MIRIN

Mirin is a sweet, fermented rice wine that is essential in Japanese cookery. Hon mirin or 'true' mirin has no added salt or sweeteners and is naturally fermented. Aji mirin, or 'seasoning' mirin has a much lower alcohol content and is usually sweetened with corn syrup. I prefer hon mirin, but it is more expensive.

MISO PASTE

Miso paste is a fermented ingredient used commonly in Japan. It's made from fermented soy beans, sometimes with rice, barley and wheat. By cooking with different types of miso, I've found that hatcho miso has a stronger flavour and darker appearance than white (shiro) miso. It is made only from soybeans and fermented for up to three years, as opposed to white miso that is made from soybeans fermented with rice for a much shorter time. You can find hatcho miso online, or you can replace it with red miso. Red miso is fermented longer than white miso, but for a shorter period than hatcho miso.

MUSHROOM STOCK POWDER

Used in the same way as chicken powder, mushroom stock powder gives a more earthy flavour. It's great to use when seasoning vegetarian dishes and adding some umami depth.

NAM PRIK PAO

Nam prik pao is a type of Thai chilli paste made from dry roasted chillies and shrimp paste. I've learned that 'nam prik' refers to a wide range of seasoning pastes used in Thai cuisine, with nam prik pao being one of the most frequently used.

NEUTRAL OIL

Throughout this book, recipes will call for neutral oil – this is any oil that has a neutral flavour, or no flavour at all. Examples include rapeseed oil, groundnut oil, vegetable oil and sunflower oil among others.

OYSTER SAUCE

Oyster sauce is a mild, sweet and well-rounded all-purpose seasoning sauce commonly used in Chinese cookery. It's made using oyster extract; however, it doesn't taste strongly of oysters or of fish. My favourite brand is Lee Kum Kee. Thai oyster sauce has a very different flavour, however – the oyster flavour is much more pronounced but overall it is less salty and slightly sweeter. For Thai recipes, I would recommend the MaeKrua brand.

PALM SUGAR

Palm sugar has a complex, deep and distinct flavour, far different to white sugar thanks to minimal processing. This also means it has more micronutrients.

PIXIAN DOUBANJIANG

Doubanjiang, or Sichuan chilli bean paste, is an intensely flavoured paste I've come to love, made from fermented broad beans and chillies. Pixian doubanjiang is the version from Pixian in the Sichuan province of China, which is famous for its chilli bean pastes, and is becoming easier to find outside China.

ROASTED CHILLI POWDER

Roasted chilli powder, or *prik bon*, is widely used by Thai cooks, and I now use it frequently in my own kitchen. It is quick and simple to make (page 18).

TOASTED SESAME OIL

Pure toasted sesame oil is more expensive than the blended sesame oil that you may be familiar with, however, it's much stronger. A small bottle will go a long way. The burning point of toasted sesame oil is quite low, so don't use it for cooking – it burns quickly and will ruin the flavour of your dish. Use it in sauces and dressings. My favourite brand is Kadoya.

SESAME SEEDS

You'll find sesame seeds used frequently in these pages and if I call for toasted, that simply requires you to toast them in a dry frying pan (skillet) over a medium heat, stirring occasionally, for 3–5 minutes or until they are golden. This is a step that helps to deepen their nutty flavour.

SHAOXING RICE WINE

Shaoxing or shoahsing wine is probably the most famous Chinese rice wine. It's an amber-coloured fermented rice wine with a complex sweet and dry flavour and, I've learned, is commonly served as a drink at the beginning of a meal. It's used in a wide range of Chinese recipes and has many culinary uses. My favourite brand is Taijade.

SICHUAN CHILLI OIL

Sichuan chilli oil has a distinct full-bodied flavour and mouth-numbing spiciness. I now know that it's the perfect addition to dumpling and noodle dishes. I have a recipe in *Dumplings and Noodles*, but if you don't want to make it yourself, there are many amazing brands to try – my favourite is CLH.

SICHUAN PEPPERCORNS

Sichuan peppercorns have become one of my favourite ingredients. They add a characteristic numbing and tingling sensation known as *mālà*, or 'numbing and spicy'. Look for *da hong pao* Sichuan peppercorns from the Gansu province in Northwest China – they will be a bright shade of reddish pink and have a fresh citrusy fragrance. To make the most of their full flavour, grind them in a pestle and mortar or spice grinder and then sieve (strain) them. This removes larger parts of the husk and inner seed, which can feel gritty. You can do this in small batches and store in an airtight jar – the peppercorn powder will remain fragrant for a week or so but will eventually lose its zing.

SOY SAUCE

Soy sauce is made from fermenting soybeans – it's a process that takes months or even years in some cases. I've found that there are many varieties, differing from brand to brand, region to region, and country to country. Usually, higher quality and artisan soy sauces will be fermented for years and aged. The older the soy sauce, the more it is prized. When a recipe calls for 'soy sauce' it will usually be referring to light soy sauce, or regular soy sauce. Light soy sauce is used to season. It adds salt and umami depth. It cannot be used interchangeably with dark soy sauce, which is darker (obviously), thicker and slightly sweeter and is used to add depth, flavour and colour. Other recipes might call for a specific soy sauce, for example Thai thin soy sauce, or Japanese soy sauce. Again, for the recipe to taste as it was intended, it's important to use the ingredient listed in the recipe. Thai thin soy sauce is used in the same way as Chinese light soy sauce, but the flavour is wildly different. My favourite brand of Chinese soy sauce is Pearl River Bridge. Healthy Boy is my go-to Thai brand (especially orange label Thai black soy sauce and green label Thai seasoning sauce), and Kikkoman is my favourite Japanese brand.

VEGETARIAN STIR FRY SAUCE

Also commonly referred to as vegetarian oyster sauce, this condiment utilizes the umami properties of shiitake mushrooms and, as I've learned through experimenting, can be used instead of oyster sauce with near-perfect results. Lee Kum Kee (the inventors of the original oyster sauce!) is a great brand to use.

STOCK CUBES

For any of these recipes, if you aren't using a homemade broth or stock, and opt instead for a stock cube, use one with low salt or no salt. This will prevent the dish from becoming over-seasoned.

SUI MI YA CAI

This is a Sichuanese speciality of finely chopped pickled mustard greens and has a distinctive sour and salty taste. You can find it in East and Southeast Asian supermarkets and online.

THE WONDER OF MSG

MSG, or monosodium glutamate, has become an essential ingredient in my kitchen and is used widely in the recipes in this book. It's used to enhance the flavour of food, much like salt, and the brand you'll most commonly come across is Ajinomoto, from Japan. Some associate MSG with a bad reputation – this is linked to an article published in the 1960s that has since been disproven many times over. Glutamates are found naturally in a wide range of ingredients, such as mushrooms and tomatoes. In 1908, its synthetic powdered form was created in Japan and this is what we use today. You can read more about MSG on *knowmsg.com*.

Key

V · vegetarian
VG · vegan

The Building Blocks

These recipes have become the cornerstones of my home-cooking repertoire. I always try to have one or all of them squirreled away in the fridge or freezer, ready to use at a moment's notice, the perfect base to build on or build a meal around.

Roasted Chilli Powder

VG · MAKES 5 TBSP · **PREP** 5 MINS · **COOKING** 5 MINS
STORE UP TO 4 WEEKS IN A COOL DARK PLACE

2 handfuls of dried red bird's eye chillies

NOTE
This method can create a very spicy gas in the air, so make sure all of your windows are open, the kitchen door is closed and no children or pets are around.

The remarkable flavour of roasted chilli powder, or *prik bon*, comes from dry roasting dried chillies, which gives a nutty and spicy aroma.

Heat a non-stick frying pan (skillet) over a medium-high heat and add the chillies. Toast on all sides until they turn a deep brown (not black) colour, keeping them moving to avoid burning.

Remove from the heat and allow to cool before transferring to a high-speed blender or use a pestle and mortar. Grind until the chillies form flakes. Store in an airtight jar.

Málà Paste

MAKES APPROX. 500ML (17FL OZ) · **PREP** 10 MINS · **COOKING** 5 MINS
STORE UP TO 2 WEEKS IN THE FRIDGE OR FREEZE IN AN ICE-CUBE TRAY

3 shallots, sliced
1 garlic head, peeled
1 tbsp ginger, grated
2 tbsp neutral oil
1 tbsp ground Sichuan peppercorns
3 tbsp *doubanjiang*
1 tbsp red miso paste
1 tbsp fermented black beans, rinsed
2 tbsp chopped pickled jalapeños
1 tbsp pickled jalapeño juice
1 tsp ground coriander
1 tsp ground fennel
2 tbsp Shaoxing rice wine
1 tbsp Sichuan chilli oil
½ tsp MSG
2 tbsp light soy sauce
1 tsp dark soy sauce
2 tbsp light (soft) brown sugar
1 tbsp honey
1 tbsp fish sauce
2 tbsp sesame oil

Málà means 'numbing and spicy' and the Sichuan peppercorns in this paste are where that taste sensation comes from. Málà paste is great for use as a general seasoning when something spicy and tingly is required, or as a hotpot seasoning.

Add the shallots, garlic and ginger to a blender and pulse to form a paste. Heat the oil in a heavy-based frying pan over a medium heat and fry the ginger-garlic-shallot paste for 2–3 minutes until fragrant and softened. Add the rest of the ingredients to the pan and mix. Allow the mixture to bubble for a further 2 minutes before transferring back to the blender (there's no need to wipe it out) and blitzing to a paste. Alternatively, you could use a stick blender. Store in an airtight jar in the fridge until needed.

Roasted Onion Broth

VG · **MAKES** 2L (70FL OZ) · **PREP** 30 MINS · **COOKING** 4 HOURS
STORE UP TO 4 DAYS IN THE FRIDGE OR 3 MONTHS IN THE FREEZER

2 large or 4 small onions
    (unpeeled), halved
5cm (2in) ginger, sliced into 8
1 garlic head, halved through its equator
300g (10½oz) carrots, peeled and
    chopped into large chunks
2 tbsp neutral oil
15g (½oz) dried mixed mushrooms,
    such as porcini
8 dried shiitake mushrooms
1 sheet of dried *kombu*
10cm (4in) daikon, halved
1 tbsp fine sea salt
1 tbsp black peppercorns
3 tbsp light soy sauce
3 tbsp Shaoxing rice wine
1 tbsp mushroom stock powder
3 spring onions (scallions)
2 tbsp soy sauce
20g (¾oz) coriander (cilantro) root

With the absence of meat and bones, a few clever ingredients are needed to boost the body and flavour of a vegetarian/vegan broth. Dried mushrooms and *kombu* are both naturally rich in glutamates, the building blocks of umami flavour. It was from kombu and shiitake that glutamate, guanylate and inosinate were first isolated, and the flavour compounds responsible for the umami flavour were discovered. Roasting the onions induces deep caramelization of the sugars in the onion, which add sweet and earthy notes.

Preheat the oven to 180°C/160°C fan/350°F/gas mark 4.

Toss the onions, half the ginger, the whole head of garlic, and carrots in the oil. Tip into a baking tin, placing the onions cut-side down, and roast in the oven for 1 hour or until the cut side of the onions are deeply brown and roasted.

In the meantime, fill a large stockpot with 3L (105fl oz) of water and add the other half of the ginger, along with the remaining ingredients. When the charred vegetables are ready, add them to the pot, skins included. Bring the pot to the boil, reduce the heat and leave to simmer gently for 3 hours, topping up the pot if the water level reduces too much and the veg becomes exposed.

After 3 hours, the broth should have taken on a dark brown colour. Line a sieve (strainer) with a piece of muslin (cheesecloth) and place over a large bowl. Pour the contents of the pan into the sieve and allow the stock to strain through the muslin. Do not press on the vegetables as this may cloud the broth. Discard the solids, rinse the muslin under warm water, then line the sieve again and strain the broth for a second time.

Decant the stock into 200ml (7fl oz) containers and either freeze or use straight away.

Ramen Eggs

V · **MAKES** 6 EGGS · **PREP** 5 MINS · **COOKING** 6 MINS + COOLING + CHILLING OVERNIGHT
STORE UP TO 5 DAYS IN THE FRIDGE

6 medium eggs
4 tbsp light soy sauce
4 tbsp mirin
250ml (9fl oz) dashi stock (made
    from powder) or water (cold)

Bring a pan of water to a rapid boil. Lower the eggs gently into the water and cook for exactly 6 minutes. Remove from the water and run under very cold water for 3–4 minutes or plunge into a bowl of water and ice cubes. When completely cool, peel the eggs.

Combine the soy, mirin and dashi. Submerge the eggs in the liquid and cover with baking paper. Alternatively, place the eggs in a sealable container or resealable plastic bag filled with the liquid. Leave in the fridge overnight to chill and marinate before eating. Will keep in the fridge for up to 5 days.

Chicken Broth

MAKES 2L (70FL OZ) · **PREP** 30 MINS · **COOKING** 2-3 HOURS
STORE UP TO 4 DAYS IN THE FRIDGE OR 3 MONTHS IN THE FREEZER

2kg (4lb 8oz) chicken wings
6–8 spring onions (scallions), trimmed
    and bashed
10cm (4in) ginger, bashed and
    thickly sliced
4 tbsp Shaoxing rice wine or water
500g (1lb 2oz) chicken feet
4 dried shiitake mushrooms
3–4 tbsp light soy sauce
1 tsp sea salt

NOTE
If you have used two tins to cook the
chicken wings, swap them round halfway
through cooking.

**A good stock can make or break a noodle soup. This stock is deeply
flavoured, full of umami and beautiful in colour. The intense chickeny
flavour comes from a widely underutilized part of the chicken – the
humble wing. When roasted, the gelatine and fat in the bone and skin
caramelize and create that beautiful chickeny smell and taste, and
give a silky texture to the broth.**

***Chintan* simply means 'clear broth' in Japanese, while chicken *paitan*
is a thick and emulsified broth. Both methods are listed below.**

Preheat the oven to 200°C/180°C fan/400°F/gas mark 6.

Spread the chicken wings in a large roasting tin, or two smaller tins
if necessary (see note), in one even layer, making sure there is space
between the wings for air to circulate – this will ensure that there are
extra crispy and juicy bits.

Roast the wings in the oven for 30 minutes. Add the spring onions
(scallions) and ginger, and baste with the fat and juice that's collected
in the bottom of the roasting tin. Put this back in the oven to roast for
another 20 minutes, checking regularly to ensure the spring onions
don't burn.

Remove the roasting tin from the oven, and transfer the wings, spring
onions and ginger to a large stockpot. Pour in any roasting juices from the
tin, scraping every edge with a spatula to get as much as you can to add to
the pot. Place the tin over a medium heat, add the Shaoxing rice wine or
water and deglaze by swirling the liquid around and scraping up any crispy
bits that are stuck to the bottom.

Once you've cleaned the tin of crispy bits, pour the mixture into the
stockpot, add the remaining ingredients, then fill with 2½L (87fl oz)
cold water, to just cover the wings.

CHICKEN CHINTAN

Use a thermometer and bring the broth to 96°C/204°F. Without a
thermometer, this looks like a bare simmer – steam will rise from the
surface but bubbles will not be visible. Cook the broth at this temperature
for 3 hours.

Take the pot off the heat and leave it to cool slightly. Line a sieve (strainer)
with a piece of muslin (cheesecloth) and place over a large bowl. Pour the
contents of the pot into the sieve. Allow the stock to strain through the
muslin, press on the ingredients to force out all the juicy goodness.

The stock should have a glimmering layer of fat on the surface and be
a lovely, rich, light brown colour. Taste the stock and season with a little
salt, if needed.

CHICKEN PAITAN

Bring the pot to a rolling boil. The consistent agitation of the surface of the broth causes the fat to emulsify into the broth, creating a cloudy appearance. Cook like this for 2 hours, topping up the pot with 250ml (9fl oz) water each hour, or more if necessary. After 2 hours, remove the pot from the heat and let it cool. Use a stick blender to whizz up the solids, including any bones. You will be left with a thick porridge-like consistency.

Line a sieve (strainer) with a piece of muslin (cheesecloth) and place over a large bowl. Pour the contents of the pan into the sieve. Allow the stock to strain through the muslin, press on the ingredients.

Both stocks are ready to serve immediately, or you can decant into 200ml (7fl oz) containers and store in the fridge or freezer until they're ready to use. The stock will turn to jelly when chilled – this is a good thing!

Master Stock

MAKES 2L (70FL OZ) · **PREP** 20 MINS · **COOKING** 2 HOURS 30 MINS
STORE UP TO 4 DAYS IN THE FRIDGE OR 3 MONTHS IN THE FREEZER

4 tbsp neutral oil
500g (1lb 2oz) beef shin (or any
    slow-braise cut), chopped into
    5cm (2in) cubes
1 garlic head, halved through its equator
5cm (2in) ginger, bashed
1 leek, cleaned and sliced into
    5cm (2in) pieces
1kg (2lb 4oz) beef marrow bones
350ml (12fl oz) Shaoxing rice wine
250g (9oz) chicken feet or wings
2L (70fl oz) water
500ml (17fl oz) light soy sauce
150g (5½oz) light (soft) brown sugar
1 tsp fennel seeds
1 tbsp coriander seeds
4 bay leaves
2 cloves
2 star anise
1 cassia bark stick
dried tangerine peel (optional)

This broth is my interpretation of a Chinese-style master stock. It is dark, rich and sweet and can be used in broths, sauces and as a marinade. In Chinese cookery, it is known as 'lo shui' or 'old water' as typically, the pot of _lo shui_ would never be replaced, but only topped up, so the flavours of multiple meats poached within it would impart their juices and fats, making the flavour of the broth richer over time.

Heat the oil in a large stockpot, over a medium-high heat. Fry the beef shin until browned on all sides. Add the garlic, ginger and leek and fry until aromatic. Add the beef bones and stir, coating them in the oil and aromatics. Add the Shaoxing rice wine and let the alcohol bubble away for 2 minutes or so, scraping up any crusty bits on the bottom of the pot. Add the chicken feet or wings, water, light soy sauce and sugar.

In a separate dry frying pan (skillet), over a medium heat, toast the fennel and coriander seeds until they become fragrant. Add these to the pot with the bay leaves, cloves, star anise, cassia and tangerine peel (if using).

Bring the pot to a steady simmer and leave to bubble away gently for at least 2 hours. Pick out the pieces of beef and set aside. Strain the broth through a fine mesh sieve (strainer) lined with muslin (cheesecloth). The resulting stock should be rich and dark. Shred the beef and return to the stock. Use immediately or decant into 200ml (7fl oz) containers, or an ice-cube tray, and freeze for later use.

noodles

Ba Mee

If you've eaten street food in Thailand, it's likely you've tried *ba mee* noodles. Ba mee noodles are a thin, yellow egg noodle that are served in lots of dishes – from noodle soups to stir fries. They have a characteristic spring and bite, and are usually crinkly.

V · MAKES APPROX. 400G (14OZ) NOODLES TO SERVE 4

PREP 40 MINS + RESTING

COOKING 2 MINS

STORE UP TO 5 DAYS IN THE FRIDGE

2 egg yolks
approx. 100g (3½oz) water
¼ tsp *kansui*
½ tsp fine sea salt
275g (9¾oz) high-protein flour (11%)
potato starch or cornflour (cornstarch),
   for dusting

In a jug, weigh the egg yolks and add enough water to reach a total weight of 120ml (4¼fl oz). Add the *kansui* and salt, and stir well to combine.

Tip the flour into a large mixing bowl, pour over the yolk mixture and gradually stir to combine. Once dry straggles have formed, bring the dough together into a ball. To do this, apply pressure using the palm of your hand in a downward motion. Continue to do this until the straggles of dough are forced together to form a rough ball. Cover with a clean, damp dish towel and rest for 15 minutes.

In the meantime, set up your pasta roller. Clamp it firmly to your worktop as the dough is extremely hard.

Remove the dough from the bowl. Take a rolling pin and press firmly onto the dough, section by section, until the dough is thin enough to pass through the pasta roller on its widest setting. Pass the dough through. What will emerge may be quite rough and ragged – this is okay! If the sheet has separated, or holes have appeared, don't worry. Pass the dough through again on the widest setting and repeat this step until you have one complete sheet of dough, with no holes. Reset the pasta roller setting to the next narrowest setting. Pass the sheet of dough through. Reduce the setting once more, to the third narrowest setting. Pass the dough through.

Now fold the dough in half, lengthways, and pass through the pasta roller on the widest setting. Repeat this sheeting and folding process until you have a smooth and even-textured sheet of dough. The edges of the sheet may have become dry and cracked – this is a result of the folding – but this is okay. Gently fold the sheet of dough in half and leave to rest for 30 minutes, covered with a clean dish towel.

Once rested, unfold the dough sheet and pass through the pasta roller again to create a thin sheet – on my pasta roller this is a number 5 or 6 for a thin noodle. Then, pass the dough through the cutting attachment. Lightly dust the noodles with potato starch of cornflour (cornstarch), to keep the strands separate.

Divide the noodles into four 100g (4oz) portions. Bundle and scrunch them between your fists and then drop onto the worktop. Repeat this three or four times, until the noodles become crinkly in shape. Place in a sealed container or freezer bag. They get better with age and resting them for 24 hours will improve the texture. They are good for up to five days in the fridge but can also be enjoyed straight away.

Cook the noodles in boiling salted water for 90 seconds or until al dente. Rinse under cold water and serve in your chosen recipe.

Wholegrain Tsukemen Noodles

Tsukemen, also known as 'dipping noodles', are used in a style of ramen where the noodles are served at room temperature, with toppings, alongside a hot bowl of soup. The idea is to dip the cool noodles into the hot broth, giving a beautiful contrast in texture and heat.

Typically, tsukemen noodles are a chunkier style of noodle than a classic thin ramen noodle. The thicker, denser tsukemen noodle provides more surface area, providing a better vessel for transporting broth from bowl to mouth. In the same respect, tsukemen dipping broth is usually thicker and more concentrated in flavour as it's intended for dipping, so you will have less soup per mouthful, as opposed to ramen broth, which is intended to be slurped.

It's said that this noodle originated in the 1950s at Tokyo restaurant Taishoken, where, on hot summer days, the staff would eat cold leftover noodles, dipped in the hot fresh broth.

VG · MAKES APPROX. 280G (10OZ) NOODLES TO SERVE 4

PREP 30 MINS + RESTING

COOKING 3 MINS

STORE UP TO 5 DAYS IN THE FRIDGE

188g (6¾oz) high-protein flour (11%)
12g (¼oz) wholegrain flour
¼ tsp fine sea salt
¼ tsp *kansui*
80g (2¾oz) water
potato starch or cornflour (cornstarch),
   for dusting

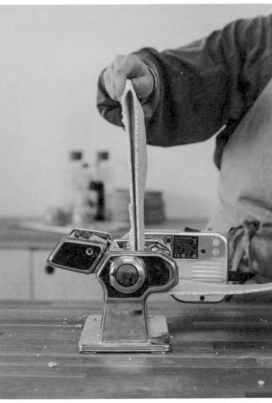

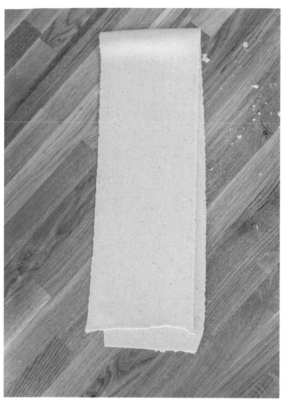

Combine the high-protein flour, wholegrain flour, salt, *kansui* and water until it starts to form dry straggles. Bring the dough together into a ball, by applying pressure using the palm of your hand in a downward motion. Continue to do this until the straggles of dough are forced together to form a rough ball. Cover with a clean, damp dish towel and rest for 15 minutes.

In the meantime, set up your pasta roller. Clamp it firmly to your worktop as the dough is extremely hard.

Remove the dough from the bowl. Take a rolling pin and press firmly onto the dough, section by section, until the dough is thin enough to pass through the pasta roller on its widest setting. Pass the dough through. What will emerge may be quite rough and ragged – this is okay! If the sheet has separated, or holes have appeared, don't worry. Pass the dough through again on the widest setting and repeat this step until you have one complete sheet of dough, with no holes. Reset the pasta roller setting to the next narrowest setting. Pass the sheet of dough through. Reduce the setting once more, to the third narrowest setting. Pass the dough through.

Now fold the dough in half, lengthways, and pass through the pasta roller on the widest setting. Repeat this sheeting and folding process until you have a smooth and even-textured sheet of dough. The edges of the sheet may have become dry and cracked – this is a result of the folding – but this is okay. Gently fold the sheet of dough in half and leave to rest for 30 minutes, covered with a clean dish towel.

Once rested, unfold the dough sheet and pass through the pasta roller again to create a sheet 3mm (⅛in) thick – on my pasta roller this is a number 3. Then, pass the dough through the cutting attachment. Lightly dust the noodles with potato starch of cornflour (cornstarch), to keep the strands separate.

Divide the noodles into four 70g (6oz) portions and place in a sealed container or freezer bag. They get better with age and resting them for 24 hours will improve the texture. They are good for up to five days in the fridge but can also be enjoyed straight away.

Cook the noodles in boiling salted water for 2–3 minutes or until al dente. Rinse in cold water and serve in your chosen recipe.

Hand-pulled Noodles

Hand-pulled noodles have various names and forms, and are common throughout China. This kind of hand-stretched noodle relies on a long autolyse, or resting period, where enzymes in the wheat digest and break bonds that form between gluten strands. This causes the dough to be extensible. The longer the dough is rested, the more stretchy the dough becomes. This differs from the popular Lanzhou *la mian* noodle, as it contains no alkali and relies only on resting to create extensibility. In Xi'an, this style of hand-pulled noodle is called *gun gun mian*, or literally 'stick' noodle, due to its thick round shape. Travel north-west from Xi'an, to Xinjiang and you will find another noodle that uses a similar technique, called *laghman* (simply meaning hand-pulled noodle, originating from 'la mian'). Some aspects of the processes will differ, such as the use of oil, or the shape in which the dough rests, but the science and method for creating extensibility in these noodles is the same.

VG · MAKES APPROX. 480G (1LB 1OZ)
NOODLES TO SERVE 4

PREP 30 MINS + RESTING

COOKING 15 MINS

320g (11¼oz) high-protein flour (11%)
160g (5½oz) water
1 tsp fine sea salt
4–5 tbsp neutral oil

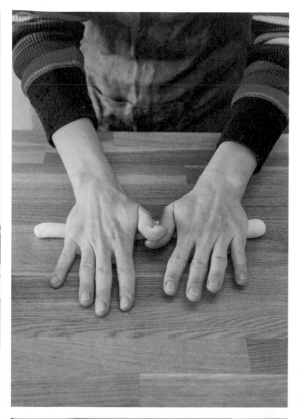

Combine the flour, water and salt until this comes together to form a dough. It may feel a little dry and crumbly at first, but don't be tempted to add more water. Knead the dough by hand or in a stand mixer for 15 minutes or until it has a smooth even texture. Portion the dough into 8 pieces, weighing 60g (2¼oz) each. Using two hands, roll each piece of dough into a long, thin sausage shape around 1–2cm (½–¾in) in diameter. Cover the dough in a liberal amount of oil before coiling it into a snail shape on a plate. Cover with clingfilm (plastic wrap) and leave to rest for 2–3 hours. Repeat with each piece of dough.

Once rested, the dough will be nice and stretchy. Bring a large pot of salted water to a rolling boil and add 1–2 tbsp oil to your worktop, before gently transferring the first dough coil.

Starting with the outer piece of dough, hold the start of the dough coil in one hand, and use the other hand to run along the length of the dough, gently pulling and stretching until the dough is 2–3mm (¹⁄₁₆–⅛in) in diameter. Drop the stretched end of the noodle directly into the boiling water. Give the pot a stir so the noodle doesn't stick to the bottom of the pan. Continue stretching the noodle until you have exhausted the dough coil. Boil for 2–3 minutes or until the noodle begins to float and has softened. Scoop the noodle out of the water and strain. Run under cold water to remove excess starch and stop the noodle from clumping. Repeat with the rest of the dough coils and serve in your chosen recipe.

Udon

Udon noodles are a Japanese thick, chewy, wheat noodle, made with just wheat flour, salt and water. They are enjoyed in various dishes, including in broth, dipped in sauce, hot and cold.

VG · MAKES APPROX. 380G (13½OZ) NOODLES TO SERVE 4

PREP 40 MINS + RESTING

COOKING 8–10 MINS

STORE UP TO 5 DAYS IN THE FRIDGE

¼ tsp fine sea salt
260g (9¼oz) high-protein flour (11%)
115g (4oz) water
potato starch or cornflour (cornstarch), for dusting

Add the salt to the flour and combine. Run chopsticks or your fingers through the flour to get rid of any large lumps. Add the water very gradually, stirring as you go, until it comes together as a ball of dough and the bowl becomes clean. You might not need all the water.

Knead the dough for 10–15 minutes. This dough is quite firm and so kneading may require some elbow grease! I stand on a chair and use my body weight to help with this, or you can do as the Japanese traditionally did (pre-stand mixers) – use your feet! If you are finding the dough too tough to knead, let it rest for 15 minutes, then come back to it. Once the dough is smooth, allow it to rest in a freezer bag or a bowl covered with a clean, damp dish towel for 30 minutes.

Take half of the dough, leaving the other half in its resting spot, and using a rolling pin, press down firmly on the dough to flatten it slightly. Roll until it's about 3mm (⅛in) thick. Ideally, the dough should be longer than it is wide but it isn't essential. This will require strength and patience! Otherwise, you can pass the dough through a pasta roller to the second or third widest setting.

Dust the dough with plenty of potato starch or cornflour (cornstarch) and roll it over four or five times, so it is around 8cm (3¼in) wide. Using a sharp knife, slice the noodles into 3mm (⅛in) pieces. Your udon noodles should have a square cross section, so they should be as wide as they are thick.

Unravel the noodles and coat in more potato starch or cornflour, then prepare the second half of the dough. Dust with a little more potato starch or cornflour and nest the noodles into 100g (3½oz) portions.

Bring a large pan of water to the boil. Shake off any excess starch from the noodle nests, drop in the pan and boil for 8–10 minutes or until they are al dente and float to the surface. Rinse with plenty of cold water to remove excess starch and stop them clumping. Serve in your chosen recipe.

NOTE
Don't be disheartened if after kneading the dough for 5 minutes, it isn't looking as it should. Keep with it! Kneading is important to evenly distribute the water through the flour and to develop the gluten. If the dough looks lumpy, it just means that the water isn't evenly distributed yet. Patience is a virtue when it comes to kneading.

Ramen

The word ramen comes from the Chinese 'la mian', which means hand-stretched noodle. Although this isn't how ramen noodles are produced now, it tells us of this noodle's history – it originated in China.

Ramen, now its own entity entirely, with its own rules, is very much rooted in Japanese culture. Ramen noodles are characterized by the addition of alkali, or *kansui*, which gives them their springy and chewy quality.

The variety of ramen noodles found in noodle shops in Japan is vast. Some thin and extremely hard, some thicker and softer, some wavy, some straight. The noodle serves as the vehicle for the soup and a true ramen master knows how to create the perfect noodle for the particular broth.

Hydration is important when it comes to ramen and this noodle comes in at 42% hydration. This means for every 100g (3½oz) of flour, we add 42g (1½oz) of water. This amount is quite high as far as ramen goes. The lower you go, the longer and harder the process. Some noodle-makers will take their hydration to as low as 30%, which results in a very taut and firm noodle.

VG · MAKES APPROX. 440G (15½OZ) NOODLES TO SERVE 4

PREP 30 MINS + RESTING

COOKING 2 MINS

STORE UP TO 5 DAYS IN THE FRIDGE

½ tsp fine sea salt
¼ tsp *kansui*
130g (4½oz) water
310g (11oz) high-protein flour (11%)
potato starch or cornflour (cornstarch), for dusting

Combine the salt, *kansui* and water, pour over the flour and mix until dry straggles have formed. Bring the dough together into a ball. To do this, apply pressure using the palm of your hand in a downward motion. Continue to do this until the straggles of dough are forced together to form a rough ball and cover with a damp dish towel, and rest for 15 minutes.

In the meantime, set up your pasta roller. Clamp it firmly to your worktop as the dough is extremely hard.

Remove the dough from the bowl. Take a rolling pin and press firmly onto the dough, section by section, until the dough is thin enough to pass through the pasta roller on its widest setting. Pass the dough through. What will emerge may be quite rough and ragged – this is okay! If the sheet has separated, or holes have appeared, don't worry. Pass the dough through again on the widest setting and repeat this step until you have one complete sheet of dough, with no holes. Reset the pasta roller setting to the next narrowest setting. Pass the sheet of dough through. Reduce the setting once more, to the third narrowest setting. Pass the dough through.

Now fold the dough in half, lengthways, and pass through the pasta roller on the widest setting. Repeat this sheeting and folding process until you have a smooth and even-textured sheet of dough. The edges of the sheet may have become dry and cracked – this is a result of the folding – but this is okay. Gently fold the sheet of dough in half and leave to rest for 30 minutes, covered with a clean dish towel.

Once rested, unfold the dough sheet and pass through the pasta roller again to create a thin sheet – on my pasta roller this is a number 5.

Pass the dough through the cutting attachment, then lightly dust the noodles with potato starch or cornflour (cornstarch) to keep the strands separate.

Place in a sealed container or freezer bag. They get better with age and resting them for 24 hours will improve the texture. They are good for up to five days in the fridge but can also be enjoyed straight away.

Cook the noodles in boiling salted water for 90 seconds. Rinse under cold water and serve in your chosen recipe.

Biang Biang

Biang biang noodles originate in Xi'an, Shaanxi province of China.

This noodle requires practice, as I've learned. The long resting time of the dough enables the enzymes in the wheat to really get to work on the gluten bonds. After 2–3 hours, the dough will be extremely elastic, allowing us to achieve a long, wavy, silky noodle. Any manipulation of the dough will mean bond formation, so it's important to handle the dough as little as possible after the resting period. Basically, you've got one chance to stretch.

The noodle will stretch to a certain point before the gluten strands begin to tighten, and you will be able to feel this after a couple of practices. The noodle will begin to tear. When the gluten begins to tighten, you need to quickly slap the noodle against the worktop – the shock temporarily halts bond formation, allowing you to stretch that little bit further. That slap is what gives this noodle its excellent name. The perfect onomatopoeia.

They must also be cooked and eaten straight after pulling. They do not sit well or travel well. The dough can be made far in advance but once pulled into a noodle, they need to go straight into a pot of boiling water, so have this ready.

VG · MAKES APPROX. 360G (12¾OZ) NOODLES TO SERVE 2

PREP 40 MINS + RESTING

COOKING 2 MINS

240g (8½oz) high-protein flour (11%)
120g (4¼oz) water
½ tsp fine sea salt
neutral oil

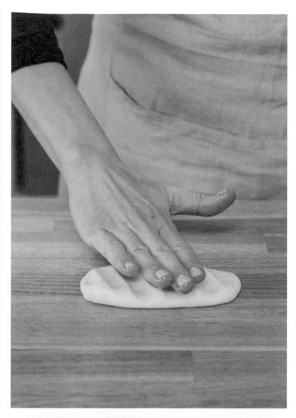

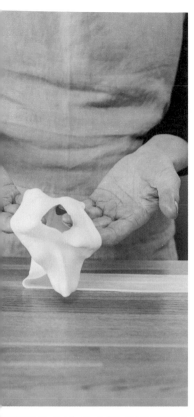

Combine the flour, water and salt until this comes together to form a dough. Knead the dough for 10 minutes or until it has a smooth even texture. Divide the dough into four 90g (3¼oz) portions and roll each into a short sausage. Place these inside a freezer bag or bowl and coat with oil. Cover and leave to rest for 2–3 hours.

Once rested, the dough will become very soft and stretchy. Rub more oil onto the worktop and gently roll the dough into an oval shape, approximately 20 x 10cm (8 x 4in). Make an indentation using your rolling pin, lengthways along the dough, being careful to not press all the way through the dough. Leave it to rest in this state for 5 minutes while you repeat the process with the remaining dough sausages.

Bring a large pan of salted water to the boil.

Pick up the rested dough oval and hold firmly at either end. Make one large pull and as the dough stretches you will feel it begin to tighten – this is usually around shoulder width. Slap it against the worktop. After each slap, make another stretch. Continue until you feel the resistance in the dough. Now tear the stretched dough in half along the indentation you made using the rolling pin and pop all the noodles into the boiling water for 1½–2 minutes or until they float. Serve in your chosen recipe.

Roast Duck Chintan Ramen

SERVES 2 · **PREP** 45 MINS · **COOKING** 4 HOURS

For the broth

1 whole duck (2-2.5kg/4lb 8oz-5lb 8oz),
   preferably with giblets (variety meats)
1 tbsp honey, mixed with 1 tbsp water
1 tbsp sea salt
400g (14oz) chicken feet
200g (7oz) daikon, cut into 5cm
   (2in) pieces
1 leek, cleaned and halved (reserving
   5cm/2in of the white part for garnish)
5cm (2in) ginger, sliced
200ml (7fl oz) Shaoxing rice wine
3 tbsp light soy sauce
3-4L (105-140fl oz) cold water

For the aromatic duck fat

1 garlic clove, grated
1 tsp ground Sichuan peppercorns,
   sieved (strained)
1 tsp onion powder

To season the bowls

2 tbsp light soy sauce
4 tsp mirin
1 tsp dashi powder
½ tsp sea salt
1 tsp freshly ground black pepper
2 tsp toasted sesame seeds
2 tsp chopped pickled jalapeños

To serve

1 ramen egg (page 19)
2 handfuls of bean sprouts
200g (7oz) fresh ramen noodles (page
   40) or 120g (4¼oz) dried ramen noodles
5cm (2in) white end of a leek, finely sliced
¼ tsp ground Sichuan peppercorns

One of my favourite parts of eating Peking duck at my favourite Chinese restaurant is the duck soup that comes alongside. The silky clear broth has a rich but light flavour and feels very nourishing and comforting.

Whenever I cook duck at home (or any bird for that matter) saving the carcass and turning it into broth comes as second nature. It is far beyond my skill set to prepare the delicate and refined duck broth that I so enjoy when eating out, but one day while I was experimenting with a roasted duck broth, I had a craving for ramen. So, this dish is a mash-up of sorts, inspired by my love of the clear and nourishing Chinese duck broth crossed with a Japanese *shoyu* ramen.

After using ingredients to make this *chintan* broth, they can be used again, to make *paitan* (page 51). The long hard boiling process softens the bones completely, releasing all their flavour and connective tissue into the stock. It's not absolutely necessary to do both – you can skip straight to the paitan here, if you wish.

It entirely depends on my mood whether I choose a clear chintan broth or a thick and creamy paitan broth. Either way, both are delicious and packed with rich duck flavour.

Preheat the oven to 200°C/180°C fan/400°F/gas mark 6.

Remove the breasts from the duck (set aside, in the fridge) and place the remaining carcass in a baking tin. Brush the duck carcass all over with the watered-down honey and season with the salt. Roast for 45 minutes or until the duck is dark and golden.

Remove from the oven and let it cool slightly before transferring to a large cutting board. Using a knife or poultry scissors, break the carcass down into four or five large pieces. Place these into a large stockpot and pour in half of the juices from the baking tin. Pour the other half into a jar or container and chill in the fridge – any debris will sink to the bottom, while delicious creamy white fat will solidify up top.

Add the chicken feet, daikon, leek, ginger, Shaoxing wine and light soy sauce to the pot. Cover the ingredients with enough cold water (3–4L/105–140fl oz) to submerge everything. Bring the pot to 96°C /204°F, if using a thermometer, or a gentle simmer, and maintain this steady, slow bubble for 3 hours. If the water level sinks so that the ingredients are exposed, top it up 200ml (7fl oz) at a time. Strain the broth through a fine mesh sieve (strainer) lined with a muslin (cheesecloth) – avoid pressing on the solids as this may cloud the broth. Discard the solids. Set aside and decant any leftovers into containers and freeze for up to 3 months.

To cook the duck breasts, place them skin-side down in a cold pan, set over a medium heat. As the heat increases, the skin will begin to render and go crisp – this should take 10 minutes or so. Flip and cook the other side for 3–4 minutes. Remove from the pan and let them rest for at least 10–15 minutes. Don't worry about them going cold, they will warm up when served in the hot broth.

Melt the solidified duck fat (discarding the debris) in a pan over a medium heat and add the garlic. Fry until it's just beginning to turn golden, then remove from the heat and add the ground Sichuan pepper and onion powder. Combine well and set aside.

Place the duck broth over a low heat to warm through. Drop the ramen egg into a mug of boiling water for 4–5 minutes to reheat. Blanch the bean sprouts in boiling water for 30 seconds. Scoop them out and set aside. In the same water, cook the ramen noodles according to the instructions on page 43 or the packet, drain and rinse with plenty of cold water, once cooked, to stop them sticking together.

Slice the rested duck breasts into 1cm (½in) slices. Take the sliced leek whites and scrunch them slightly between two hands to separate them.

To assemble, season each serving bowl with 1 tbsp light soy sauce, 2 tsp mirin, ½ tsp dashi powder, ¼ tsp salt, ½ tsp ground black pepper, 1 tsp sesame seeds and 1 tsp chopped pickled jalapeños. Add 300ml (10½fl oz) warm duck broth and stir to combine.

To each bowl, add the noodles and top with the duck breast slices, half a ramen egg, blanched bean sprouts and sliced leek whites. Drizzle over the aromatic duck fat and sprinkle over ground Sichuan peppercorns using a sieve (strainer).

NOTE
A pre-roasted whole duck carcass will work perfectly for both the duck *chintan* ramen and *paitan* ramen. A whole raw duck, fresh or frozen, works too.

Roast Duck Paitan Ramen

SERVES 2 · **PREP** 1 HOUR · **COOKING** 4–6 HOURS

For the broth

1 whole duck (2–2.5kg/4lb 8oz–5lb 8oz),
    preferably with giblets (variety meats)
1 tbsp honey, mixed with 1 tbsp water
1 tbsp sea salt
400g (14oz) chicken feet
200g (7oz) daikon, cut into 5cm
    (2in) pieces
1 leek, cleaned and halved
5cm (2in) ginger, sliced
200ml (7fl oz) Shaoxing rice wine
3 tbsp light soy sauce
1½L (52fl oz) cold water

For the aromatic duck fat

1 garlic clove, grated
1 tsp hoisin sauce
1 tsp onion powder

To season the bowls

2 tbsp light soy sauce
4 tsp mirin
1 tsp dashi powder
½ tsp sea salt
1 tsp freshly ground black pepper
4 tsp toasted sesame seeds
½ tsp onion powder

To serve

100g (3½oz) choi sum or pak choi
    (bok choy)
1 handful of bean sprouts
200g (7oz) fresh ramen noodles
    (page 40) or 120g (4¼oz) dried
    ramen noodles
1 ramen egg (page 19)
1 spring onion (scallion), finely sliced

Paitan **broth is a thick and creamy style of broth, in which a rapid boil agitates the water so much that it emulsifies the fats, creating a creamy appearance.**

Preheat the oven to 200°C/180°C fan/400°F/gas mark 6.

Remove the breasts from the duck (set aside, in the fridge) and place the remaining carcass in a baking tin. Brush the duck carcass all over with the watered-down honey and season with the salt. Roast for 45 minutes or until the duck is dark and golden.

Remove from the oven and let it cool slightly before transferring to a large cutting board. Using a knife or poultry scissors, break the carcass down into four or five large pieces. Place these into a pressure cooker or large stockpot and pour in half of the juices from the baking tin. Pour the other half into a jar or container and chill in the fridge – any debris will sink to the bottom, while delicious creamy white fat will solidify up top.

If using a pressure cooker, add the chicken feet, daikon, leek, ginger, Shaoxing wine and light soy sauce to the pot. Cover the ingredients with the cold water. Bring the pot to full pressure over a medium-high heat. Once a steady stream of steam is escaping, turn the heat down to maintain this stream. Keep the pot at this temperature for 1 hour 30 minutes. After this time, turn the heat off and allow the pot to depressurise (this can take around 10–15 minutes). Remove the lid and allow the broth the cool for a further 20 minutes. Don't skip this step as broth cooked inside a pressure cooker reaches and remains at scalding temperatures.

If cooking on the stove, add the chicken feet, daikon, leek, ginger, Shaoxing wine and light soy sauce to the stockpot. Cover the ingredients with 2½L (87fl oz) cold water. Cook for 4 hours over a high heat, at a rolling simmer. Top up the pot with water if the bones become exposed – you might have to do this a few times.

Once the broth has finished cooking, use a stick blender to blend and grind the softened carcass until it resembles a thick porridge.

Take a fine mesh sieve (strainer) lined with muslin (cheesecloth) and strain the broth two ladles at a time, pressing on the solids. There will be quite a lot of solids left, so discard these each time. Transfer the strained broth back to a large, clean saucepan and set over a low heat while you prepare the rest of the ingredients.

To cook the duck breasts, place them skin-side down in a cold pan, set over a medium heat. As the heat increases, the skin will begin to render and go crisp – this should take 10 minutes or so. Flip and cook the other side for 3–4 minutes. Remove from the pan and let them rest for at least 10–15 minutes. Don't worry about them going cold, they will warm up when served in the hot broth.

Melt the solidified duck fat (discarding the debris) in a pan over a medium heat and add the garlic. Fry until fragrant, then remove from the heat and add the hoisin sauce and onion powder, and whisk to combine (separation will occur when standing, but this is okay).

Place the duck broth over a low heat to warm through and bring another pan of salted water to the boil. Blanch the choi sum or pak choi (bok choy) and bean sprouts for 30 seconds. Scoop out and set aside. In the same pan, cook the noodles according to the instructions on page 43 or on the packet, drain and rinse with plenty of cold water, once cooked, to stop them sticking together. Place the ramen eggs in a mug of boiling water to gently reheat.

Slice the rested duck breasts into 1cm (½in) slices.

To assemble, season each serving bowl with 1 tbsp light soy sauce, 2 tsp mirin, ½ tsp dashi powder, ¼ tsp salt, ½ tsp ground black pepper, 2 tsp sesame seeds, ¼ tsp onion powder. Add 300ml (10½fl oz) hot broth and stir to combine.

To each bowl, add the noodles and top with the duck breast slices, half a ramen egg, blanched bean sprouts and leafy greens, and spring onions (scallions) and drizzle over the aromatic duck fat.

Málà Duck Tsukemen

SERVES 2 · **PREP** 15 MINS · **COOKING** 30 MINS + RESTING

For the broth

600ml (21fl oz) duck *paitan* broth (page 51)

2 tbsp *málà* paste (page 18)

½ tsp powdered gelatine

½ tsp dashi powder

To season the bowls

1 tsp sesame oil

1 tsp onion powder

2 tsp chopped pickled jalapeños

2 tbsp Sichuan chilli oil

2 tsp aromatic duck fat (page 51)

2 tbsp light soy sauce

2 tsp light (soft) brown sugar

To serve

2 duck breasts

50g (1¾oz) enoki mushrooms

140g (5oz) *tsukemen* noodles (page 28) or 100g (3½oz) dried thick wheat noodles

2 ramen eggs (page 19)

½ tsp ground nori powder

¼ tsp ground Sichuan pepper, sieved (strained)

1 spring onion (scallion), finely sliced

Tsukemen, also known as 'dipping noodles' are a style of ramen where the noodles are served room temperature, with toppings, alongside a hot bowl of soup. The idea is to dip the cool noodles into the hot broth, giving a beautiful contrast in texture and heat.

The numbing and spicy *málà* paste works beautifully with the duck broth, creating a deep, rich umami flavour and demonstrates a crossover between Sichuanese flavours in a Japanese-style dish.

To cook the duck breasts, place them skin-side down in a cold pan, set over a medium heat. As the heat increases, the skin will begin to render and go crisp – this should take 10 minutes or so. Flip and cook the other side for 3–4 minutes. Remove from the pan and let them rest for at least 10–15 minutes. Don't worry about them going cold, they will be dipped into the hot broth when served.

Add the duck broth, *málà* paste and gelatine to a saucepan, combine well and bring to the boil. Cook until the liquid has reduced slightly and thickened. Season with the dashi powder.

Put a large pan of salted water on to boil.

Once the water is boiling, blanch the enoki mushrooms for 10 seconds. Remove and set aside.

Cook the noodles according to the instructions on page 31 or on the packet, drain and rinse with plenty of cold water, once cooked, to stop them sticking together. Place the ramen eggs in a mug of boiling water to gently reheat.

Slice the rested duck breasts into 1cm (½in) slices.

To assemble, season each serving bowl with ½ tsp sesame oil, ½ tsp onion powder, 1 tsp chopped pickled jalapeños, 1 tbsp chilli oil, 1 tsp aromatic duck fat, 1 tbsp light soy sauce and 1 tsp light (soft) brown sugar. Add the hot stock and combine well. Sprinkle over the nori powder and ground Sichuan pepper.

Serve the noodles, duck, enoki, sliced spring onions (scallions) and ramen egg (halved) on a plate, on the side.

Duck Offal Biang Biang

SERVES 2 · **PREP** 40 MINS · **COOKING** 30 MINS

For the sauce
75g (2½oz) duck livers
1 tsp cornflour (cornstarch)
1 tbsp Shaoxing rice wine
2 tsp light soy sauce
2 tbsp neutral oil
1 shallot, sliced
1 tsp honey
½ tsp Chinese five spice
2–4 duck hearts
3 tbsp duck or chicken *chintan* broth
   (pages 48 and 20) or water
360g (12¾oz) biang biang noodle dough
   (page 44)

To season the bowls
2 tsp *málà* paste (page 18)
½ tsp ground Sichuan peppercorns,
   sieved (strained)
2 small pinches of MSG
1 tsp onion powder
2 tsp duck or chicken fat

To serve
200g (7oz) pak choi (bok choy), halved
1 tsp toasted sesame seeds
1 spring onion (scallion), sliced
crispy fried garlic (optional)

I absolutely love using whole duck – the meat and carcass contain so much flavourful fat, and the bold flavour can stand up to so many seasonings. The whole frozen ducks I usually buy come with a sachet containing the giblets – that is, the heart, liver and neck. I include the neck in my stock pot, but the heart and liver are of no use when it comes to stock making. Not wanting them to go to waste, I use them to create a rich and spicy dressing for biang biang noodles.

Prepare the duck livers by removing any fatty sinew. Combine the cornflour (cornstarch), Shaoxing rice wine, 1 tsp of the light soy sauce and mix. Add the duck livers and toss to coat. Heat the oil in a non-stick frying pan (skillet) or wok and fry the livers for 1–2 minutes on either side. Remove and drain on paper towels. Fry the shallots until golden brown and drain on paper towels. Set aside.

Combine the remaining 1 tsp light soy sauce, the honey and Chinese five spice. Add the duck hearts and toss to coat. Leave to marinate while you prepare the rest of the dish.

Bring the duck broth (or water) to a simmer.

Finely chop the duck livers and divide between two serving bowls. To each bowl, add 1 tsp *málà* paste, ¼ tsp ground Sichuan peppercorns, 1 small pinch of MSG, ½ tsp onion powder and 1 tsp duck or chicken fat. Divide the crispy shallots between each bowl. Add the hot stock and mash the liver with the back of a fork to create a chunky sauce.

Heat a frying pan or griddle pan to smoking point. Add the duck hearts and cook for 2 minutes on each side or until caramelized and golden. Slice in half lengthways.

Blanch the pak choi (bok choy) in boiling salted water for 2 minutes, scoop out and set aside. Keep the pan on to boil.

Pull and cook the biang biang noodles according to the instructions on page 47 and transfer straight from the pan into the duck liver sauce. Top with the choi sum, duck hearts, sesame seeds, spring onions (scallions) and crispy fried garlic, if using.

Thai Beef Short Rib Noodles

SERVES 6 · **PREP** 15 MINS · **COOKING** 4 HOURS 15 MINS

For the broth

6 garlic cloves, peeled
100g (3½oz) coriander (cilantro) root
2 tsp white peppercorns
4 tbsp neutral oil
1.8kg (4lb) beef short rib (or 6 short ribs, bone in), or 1.2kg (2lb 12oz) beef shin
1kg (2lb 4oz) meaty beef bones/beef marrow bones
200ml (7fl oz) Shaoxing rice wine
4L (140fl oz) water
500g (1lb 2oz) chicken feet (or chicken wings)
4 star anise
4 bay leaves
2 cassia bark stick
1 tsp allspice berries (optional)
75g (2½oz) *galangal*, finely sliced
5 dried shiitake mushrooms
100g (3½oz) palm sugar
250ml (9fl oz) light soy sauce (Thai thin soy sauce works best)
250ml (9fl oz) Thai seasoning sauce
2 tbsp Thai black soy sauce

To season the bowls

6 tbsp lime juice
4 tbsp Thai fish sauce
¾ tsp MSG

To serve

6 handfuls of bean sprouts
200g (7oz) morning glory, cut into 5cm (2in) pieces
600g (1lb 5oz) fresh *ba mee* noodles (page 24) or 300g (10½oz) dried egg noodles
200g (7oz) beef tendon balls or beef balls
3 small handfuls of coriander (cilantro), roughly chopped
3 small handfuls of Thai basil, leaves picked
2 tbsp roasted chilli powder (page 18)

This dish is inspired by an infinitely bubbling beef hotpot I tasted in Bangkok, which came with fresh, thin *ba mee* noodles, served in a flaming hotpot with offal (variety meats), tripe and beef balls. The pot, the chef said, was always boiling – with new stock and meat being added each day. This meant that the pot itself was seasoning the dish, with a rich and fragrant layer of fat contrasting with the textural bite from the frilly tripe, making it completely inimitable. I dreamt of that dish often when I got home and did my best to recreate it. It's never matched the same standard, but I enjoy it nonetheless.

Bash the garlic, coriander (cilantro) root and white peppercorns in a pestle and mortar, or in a mini blender, until they form a rough paste and the fragrance begins to waft into the air.

Heat the oil in a large stockpot, over a medium-high heat. Fry the beef on all sides until brown, then remove from the pan and set aside. Fry the aromatic paste in the same pan for 1 minute or until fragrant. Add the meaty bones and toss to coat in the aromatic paste. Pour in the Shaoxing rice wine and let the alcohol bubble away, for 2 minutes. Add the water, chicken feet and browned short ribs or beef shin. Add the remaining aromatics and seasonings. Bring the pot to a slow and steady simmer and leave for 3–4 hours, checking every now and again on the water level. If the bones become exposed, top up with water until they are submerged again.

After 3–4 hours, there should be a thick layer of dark fat on top of the broth (save this – it's delicious) and the meat should be soft and melting. Scoop out the meat, and allow to cool slightly before shredding or roughly chopping and setting to one side. Strain the remaining broth through a fine mesh sieve (strainer) lined with muslin (cheesecloth) – avoid pressing on the veg/debris as this will cause the broth to become cloudy. Discard the solids. Clean the pan, before returning the broth to the pan to gently heat.

Put a large pan of salted water on to boil.

Blanch the bean sprouts and morning glory in the boiling water for 30 seconds. Scoop them out and set aside. In the same water, cook the noodles until al dente according to the instructions on page 27 or on the packet. Scoop out, and then rinse in plenty of cold water until they are completely cool – this will prevent them from sticking – then set aside. In the same water, boil the beef tendon balls or beef balls for 5 minutes, drain and set aside.

To assemble, season each serving bowl with 1 tbsp lime juice, 2 tsp fish sauce and ⅛ tsp MSG, then add 300ml (10½fl oz) steaming stock. Stir to combine. Add noodles and top with the blanched bean sprouts, shredded beef, morning glory, beef balls and fresh herbs. Finish with a sprinkle of roasted chilli powder.

Aromatic Jackfruit Noodle Soup

V · SERVES 4 · **PREP** 10 MINS · **COOKING** 1 HOUR 20 MINS

3 garlic cloves, peeled

40g (1½oz) coriander (cilantro) root

1 tsp white peppercorns

4 tbsp neutral oil

2 x 565g (1lb 4oz) tins young green jackfruit, drained

4 tbsp Shaoxing rice wine

2L (70fl oz) roasted onion broth (page 19)

2 star anise

2 bay leaves

1 cassia bark stick

30g (1oz) *galangal*, finely sliced

2 dried shiitake mushrooms

50g (1¾oz) palm sugar

125ml (4fl oz) light soy sauce (Thai thin soy sauce works best)

125ml (4fl oz) Thai seasoning sauce

1 tbsp Thai black soy sauce

To season the bowls

4 tbsp lime juice

8 tsp vegetarian oyster sauce

½ tsp MSG

To serve

2 tbsp neutral oil

1 tbsp butter or vegan butter

250g (9oz) shimeji mushrooms

1 tsp sea salt

1 tsp light (soft) brown sugar

200g (7oz) morning glory, cut into 5cm (2in) pieces

4 handfuls of bean sprouts

400g (14oz) *ba mee* noodles (page 24) or 200g (7oz) dried thin egg noodles

1 small handful of coriander (cilantro), roughly chopped

1 small handful of Thai basil, leaves picked

1 tsp roasted chilli powder (page 18)

This dish is the vegetarian riff on my favourite Thai beef broth. My partner is vegetarian, so I'm often finding ways to prepare my favourite recipes without meat.

Bash the garlic, coriander (cilantro) root and white peppercorns in a pestle and mortar, or in a mini blender, until they form a rough paste and the fragrance begins to waft into the air.

Heat the oil in a large stockpot, over a medium-high heat, add the aromatic paste and fry for 1 minute or until it is fragrant. Add the jackfruit and toss to coat in the aromatic paste. Pour in the Shaoxing rice wine and let the alcohol bubble away, for 2 minutes. Add the onion broth and all the aromatics and seasonings. Bring to a slow simmer and cook for 1 hour. Remove the bay leaves, star anise, cassia bark and *galangal* and discard.

Meanwhile, heat the oil and butter in a large heavy-based frying pan (skillet) over a medium heat. Add the mushrooms and salt, making sure there is plenty of room in between each mushroom – if the pan is overcrowded, the mushrooms will boil and become slimy. Toss to coat the mushrooms in the oil and leave to brown. Add the sugar and turn the heat to the lowest setting. Stir the mushrooms once more to coat and cook for 5–6 minutes or until caramelized. Do not be tempted to stir them too much. Toss in the pan and continue to cook over a low heat until they're darkly caramelized. Remove from the heat and set aside.

In a pan of boiling salted water, blanch the morning glory for 30 seconds, scoop out and set aside. Blanch the bean sprouts for 1 minute, scoop out and set aside. In the same pan, cook the noodles according to their instructions on page 27 or on the packet, drain and rinse in plenty of cold water and set aside.

To assemble, season each serving bowl with 1 tbsp lime juice, 2 tsp oyster sauce and a sprinkle of MSG. Add 300ml (10½fl oz) hot broth. To each bowl, add the noodles and top with 4–5 pieces of jackfruit, caramelized mushrooms, morning glory, bean sprouts, coriander (cilantro) and Thai basil. Finish with a dusting of roasted chilli powder.

Roasted Broccoli Drunkard's Noodles

SERVES 2 · **PREP** 30 MINS · **COOKING** 20 MINS

100g (3½oz) long-stemmed broccoli
3 tbsp neutral oil
200g (7oz) dried wide rice noodles
1 tbsp sesame oil
3 garlic cloves, sliced
1 large red chilli, sliced
1 red bird's eye chilli, sliced
1 tsp sea salt
200g (7oz) large shell-on tiger
   or king prawns (jumbo shrimp)
1 tbsp Shaoxing rice wine
½ red onion, finely sliced
½ red (bell) pepper, finely sliced
1 handful of Thai basil leaves

For the sauce
3 tbsp Thai oyster sauce
1 tbsp Thai fish sauce
1 tbsp Thai thin soy sauce
1 tbsp light (soft) brown sugar
½ tsp dark soy sauce
2 tbsp warm water

Drunkard's noodles are said to have begun life as an aromatic meat-based stir fry and were commonly served alongside alcohol within Thai drinking circles, and so were called *pad kra-pao*, aka drunkard's stir fry. Later, noodles were added, drunkard's noodles were born and have since become popular around the world.

Usually, Thai holy basil would be used here – it's different to Thai basil, being more peppery. However, holy basil can be hard to come by outside of Thailand, so I use Thai basil here.

Beef, chicken or pork are also typical, however, I was making this dish with prawns (shrimp) and leftover vegetables one day for my daughter's lunch and I found the umami crunch of the broccoli worked really well among the slick, anise-spiked noodles, and this adaptation became a staple.

Preheat the oven to 200°C/180°C Fan/400°F/gas mark 6.

Place the broccoli on a baking sheet and rub with 1 tbsp neutral oil. Roast in the oven for 15–20 minutes or until slightly charred. Remove and set aside.

Meanwhile, soak the rice noodles in boiling water for 15 minutes until softened but still al dente. Strain and rinse under plenty of cold water to stop them sticking together. Add the sesame oil and toss to coat.

With a pestle and mortar, bash the garlic, chillies and salt to form a chunky paste.

Combine the ingredients for the sauce with 2 tbsp warm water. Stir to dissolve the sugar.

When you're ready to cook, heat 2 tbsp neutral oil in a wok over a high heat. Add the garlic-chilli paste and stir quickly for 20 seconds. Add the prawns (jumbo shrimp) and stir to coat in the garlic and chilli. Add the Shaoxing rice wine and allow to bubble for 1–2 minutes. Add the broccoli, red onion and red (bell) pepper, keeping everything moving in the wok. Cook for 1 minute before adding the softened noodles. Toss everything together, add the sauce and mix well to coat. Cook for a further 2–3 minutes or until the sauce is reduced slightly and absorbed.

Remove from the heat and throw in the Thai basil leaves. Toss through the noodles until wilted.

Tom Yam Noodle Soup

SERVES 4 · **PREP** 25 MINS · **COOKING** 40 MINS

For the broth

8 large, head-on, shell-on tiger
  or king prawns (jumbo shrimp)
1 tbsp neutral oil
1L (35fl oz) chicken *chintan* broth
  (page 20)
6 lime leaves, torn and bruised
2 lemongrass stalks, bashed
10cm (4in) *galangal*, finely sliced
1 red bird's eye chilli (optional
  – if you like it spicy)
325g (11½oz) baby plum tomatoes
300g (10½oz) oyster or shimeji
  mushrooms
2 tbsp palm sugar
2 tbsp *nam prik pao*
4 tbsp fish sauce
410g (14½oz) evaporated milk

To season the bowls

4 tbsp lime juice
2 tsp caster (superfine) sugar
4 tsp fish sauce

To serve

400g (14oz) *ba mee* noodles (page 24)
  or 200g (7oz) dried thin egg noodles
1 small handful of coriander (cilantro),
  roughly chopped
1 small handful of Thai basil leaves,
  leaves picked (optional)

NOTE

Bashing and crunching the aromatics
prior to adding them to the broth helps
to release those aromatic compounds
that we love. They should be brewed
gently, as if brewing a tea, to impart their
flavour into the broth.

There are many, many iterations of this Thai soup. This version likely
represents the flavour of *tom yam* soup that you might know well and
has become familiar through Thai restaurants outside of Thailand.
Traditionally, evaporated milk would not have been added. Yet, in
recent history this became popular and is now used by street vendors
all over Bangkok.

I love the addition of Thai basil, but this is by no means common.

Remove the heads from the prawns (jumbo shrimp), by twisting and pulling
the heads away from the bodies, and set aside. Remove the shells by
cutting along the back of the shell with some kitchen scissors to reveal the
black intestinal tract. Remove this with a toothpick and discard. Peel back
the shells and add to the pile of heads, and set the prawn meat to one side.

Add the prawn heads and shells and the neutral oil to a large saucepan set
over a medium heat. Fry until they are red and fragrant, crushing them with
a potato masher or the back of a fork. Add the chicken broth and scrape
up any crusty bits from the bottom of the pan. Bring the mix to a gentle
simmer. Add the lime leaves, lemongrass, *galangal* and whole chilli, if using.
Let the broth simmer very gently like this for 5–10 minutes – any longer and
you'll overcook these delicate aromatics. Strain through a fine mesh sieve
(strainer) lined with muslin (cheesecloth) and return the broth to the pan.

Add the tomatoes, mushrooms and palm sugar and simmer gently for 3–4
minutes or until the sugar has dissolved. Turn the heat to the lowest setting
and add the *nam prik pao*, fish sauce and evaporated milk. Stir to combine.
Add the prawns and let them cook gently for 1–2 minutes or until they are
just pink. Once cooked, scoop the prawns out of the broth and set aside.

Put a large pan of salted water on to boil.

Cook the noodles according to their instructions on page 27 or on
the packet, drain and rinse in plenty of cold water and set aside.

To assemble, season each serving bowl with 1 tbsp lime juice, ½ tsp sugar
and 1 tsp fish sauce. Add 300ml (10½fl oz) hot stock, dividing the tomatoes
and mushrooms evenly between the bowls, and stir to combine. Sit the
ba mee noodles in the middle and top with prawns, coriander (cilantro)
and Thai basil, if using.

Spicy Chicken & Crab Tsukemen

SERVES 2 · **PREP** 15 MINS · **COOKING** 1 HOUR 15 MINS

For the chashu chicken

1 tbsp neutral oil
2 skinless chicken thighs
80ml (2½fl oz) sake
80ml (2½fl oz) light soy sauce
80ml (2½fl oz) mirin
2 tbsp light (soft) brown sugar
200ml (7fl oz) water
2 spring onions (scallions), chopped
    into 5cm (2in) pieces
2½cm (1in) ginger, sliced

To season the bowls

2 tbsp light soy sauce
4 tsp mirin
4 tsp sake
2 tsp light (soft) brown sugar
1 tsp chicken powder (see note
    on page 13)
2 tbsp *gochujang*

To serve

650ml (22fl oz) chicken *paitan* broth
    (page 51)
140g (5oz) *tsukemen* noodles
    (page 28) or 100g (3½oz) dried thick
    wheat noodles
6 tbsp brown and white crab meat
1 small handful of chives, finely sliced
1 toasted nori sheet, halved lengthways

This bowl perfectly balances rich chicken and light fresh crab.

Preheat the oven to 150°C/130°C fan/300°F/gas mark 2.

Heat the oil in a large ovenproof frying pan (skillet) over a medium-high heat. Brown the chicken thighs on both sides. Add the sake, light soy sauce, mirin, sugar and water. Add the spring onions (scallions) and ginger. Tightly cover with two layers of foil and cook in the oven for 1 hour or until the chicken is meltingly soft.

Warm the broth over a gentle heat.

Put a large pan of salted water on to boil.

Cook the noodles according to the instructions on page 31 or on the packet, drain and rinse with plenty of cold water to stop them from sticking together.

To assemble, season each serving bowl with 1 tbsp light soy sauce, 2 tsp mirin, 2 tsp sake, 1 tsp light (soft) brown sugar, ½ tsp chicken powder and 1 tbsp *gochujang*. Add 300ml (10½fl oz) hot chicken *paitan* broth to each bowl, stir to combine and dissolve the gochujang. Divide the crab meat between the bowls, placing it on the surface of the broth and sprinkle with the chopped chives. On a separate plate, add the *tsukemen* noodles and chicken *chashu*. Finally, prop the toasted nori against the edge of the bowl with the bottom 1cm (½in) dipped in the broth.

Tonkotsu Tsukemen

SERVES 6 (WITH LEFTOVER BROTH) · **PREP** 45 MINS · **COOKING** 3½–6½ HOURS

For the broth
1kg (2lb 4oz) pork bones
1½kg (3lb 5oz) chicken wings
500g (1lb 2oz) chicken feet
700g–1kg (1lb 9oz–2lb 4oz) pork belly,
  skin separated
1cm (½in) ginger, sliced
10 garlic cloves, peeled
1 large onion, quartered

For the chashu pork
1 tbsp neutral oil
80ml (2½fl oz) sake
80ml (2½fl oz) light soy sauce
80ml (2½fl oz) mirin
2 tbsp light (soft) brown sugar
200ml (7fl oz) water
2 spring onions (scallions)
2½cm (1in) ginger, sliced

Katsuobushi salt
2 tbsp *katsuobushi*
1 tbsp sea salt

To season the bowls
6 tbsp light soy sauce
4 tbsp mirin
4 tbsp sake
3 tsp dashi powder
1½ tsp *katsuobushi* salt
6 tsp light (soft) brown sugar
1½ tsp onion powder

This bowl is a homemade recreation of one of my most memorable meals in Japan, at a restaurant specializing in award-winning *tsukemen*, named Fūunji in Shinjuku. I craved it daily once I returned home. The broth was thick and grey, topped with a small mound of ground *katsuobushi*. The noodles were thick and bouncy with a perfect amount of resistance and chew. Most memorable of all was the charismatic head chef Miyake whose serving skills were more like performance art. The experience of eating this at home is different, but the flavours are as true to the original as I could manage. You can make it on the stove or in a pressure cooker.

Add the pork bones, chicken wings, chicken feet and pork belly skin to a large stockpot and cover with cold water. Bring to a rapid boil and cook for 3–5 minutes or until a lot of scum and foam has formed on the surface. Carefully tip the bones into a colander and discard the water. Wash and rinse the bones under cold water, removing any dried blood, dirt or debris.

If using a pressure cooker, add the pork bones, chicken feet and wings, and pork belly skin to the pot and cover with 4L (140fl oz) water. Cook at high pressure for 2 hours. Release the pressure and add the ginger, garlic and onion. Boil uncovered for a further 1 hour.

If cooking on the stove, add the pork bones, chicken feet and wings, and pork belly skin back to the large stockpot and cover with 4L (140fl oz) water. Cook for 6 hours over a high heat, at a rolling simmer. Top up the pot with water if the bones become exposed – you might have to do this a few times. After 5 hours, add the ginger, garlic and onion and continue boiling for 1 more hour.

Meanwhile, preheat the oven to 120°C/100°C fan/250°F/gas mark ½.

$\longrightarrow$

Heat the oil in a large ovenproof frying pan (skillet) over a medium-high heat. Brown the pork belly on all sides. Remove to a plate. Add the sake, light soy sauce, mirin, sugar and water to the frying pan and heat gently, scraping any bits from the bottom of the pan into the sauce. Add the spring onions (scallions) and ginger and return the pork to the pan, turning to coat in the sauce. Tightly cover with two layers of foil and cook in the oven for 3 hours or until meltingly soft. Allow the pork to cool before transferring to a container, along with all the cooking liquor. Place in the fridge to chill – this makes it easier to slice.

Once the broth has finished cooking, most of the bones should have softened. If there are any large robust bones that are still solid, remove these and discard. Allow the stock to cool. Use a stick blender to blitz up the veg and softened bones, to form a chunky, porridge-like broth. Line a fine mesh sieve (strainer) with muslin (cheesecloth) and strain the broth, pressing on the pulp and debris to extract as much liquid as possible. Decant into a container and store in the fridge until ready to use. The broth is best served the next day (see page 10 for the science!), but it can be used straight away, if you like.

Grind the salt and *katsuobushi* flakes using a pestle and mortar to a coarse powder. Set aside.

When you're ready to serve, warm 1¾L (61fl oz) broth in a pan set over a medium heat. Add the ramen eggs to a jug of boiling water to gently reheat.

Slice the *chashu* pork into 5mm (¼in) slices. Add the pork cooking liquor and pork slices to a large, deep frying pan set over a medium heat and gently warm through.

Put a large pan of salted water on to boil.

Cook the noodles according to the instructions on page 31 or on the packet, drain and rinse with plenty of cold water, once cooked, to stop them sticking together.

Divide the noodles between six serving plates or bowls, along with 100g (3½oz) pork and ½ a ramen egg each, and a scattering of spring onions (scallions).

To assemble, season each serving bowl with 1 tbsp light soy sauce, 2 tsp mirin, 2 tsp sake, ½ tsp dashi powder, ¼ tsp katsuobushi salt, 1 tsp light (soft) brown sugar and ¼ tsp onion powder. Add 300ml (10½fl oz) hot stock to each bowl and stir to combine. Prop the toasted nori against the edge of the bowl with the bottom 1cm (½in) dipped in the broth. Top each broth with a small pile of ½ tsp katsuobushi salt and serve alongside the noodle plates.

To serve

420g (15oz) *tsukemen* noodles (page 28) or 300g (10½oz) dried thick wheat noodles

3 ramen eggs (page 19)

4 spring onions (scallions), finely shredded and placed into a bowl of ice water

2 toasted nori sheets, each sheet divided into 6 pieces

Lanzhou-style Beef Noodles

SERVES 6 · **PREP** 1 HOUR · **COOKING** 3 HOURS 30 MINS

For the broth

1kg (2lb 4oz) meaty beef bones

300g (10½oz) oxtail

800g (1lb 12oz) beef shin or stewing beef

1 tbsp Sichuan peppercorns

4cm (1½in) cassia bark stick

1 tsp clove

1 tbsp fennel seeds

3 star anise

4 bay leaves

1 black cardamom pod

6 pieces sand ginger
   (see note on page 72)

5 slices liquorice root
   (see note on page 72)

2 tbsp sea salt

10cm (4in) ginger, sliced

5 spring onions (scallions), white part
   bashed, green part finely sliced

4L (140fl oz) cold water

10cm (4in) daikon, quartered and
   sliced into 2mm (⅛in) pieces

To season the bowls

¾ tsp fine sea salt

¾ tsp MSG

1½ tsp light (soft) brown sugar

To serve

720g (1lb 9oz) hand-pulled noodles
   (page 32) or 400g (14oz) round thick
   wheat noodles

6 tbsp Sichuan chilli oil or Lao Gan
   Ma Crispy Chilli Oil

2 small handfuls of coriander (cilantro),
   roughly chopped

For most of the inhabitants of Lanzhou, the capital city of North-western China's Gansu province, a typical day will begin with a bowl of clear and fragrant beef broth and Lanzhou *la mian* (hand-pulled) noodles. Huge, steaming bowls of the stuff are served from more than 20,000 beef noodle shops every day, assembled from start to finish in under 30 seconds flat.

I was lucky enough to visit Lanzhou noodle school and train there for a few days while in China. To achieve the recognized qualification, the course is 30 days long. This qualification enables graduates to open their own noodle shop; however, it is no easy feat to attain. The day is long and includes hard, manual labour, where up to 6 hours of the day alone will be spent kneading dough in order to learn the correct consistency for pulling noodles. Students sleep on site in dorms and often stay on to practise long after the end of the school day so it really is a full-time undertaking to achieve this renowned qualification. The curriculum focuses on la mian, making of the broth and perfecting the chilli oil.

To make the noodles correctly requires expert tuition, a lot of practise and a specific alkaline substance found in Northwestern China, called *penghui*. Derived from the native desert plant *penghuicao* (*Halogen arachoideus*), usually referred to as 'ash' at noodle school, penghui is not available outside of China. And so, here I have replaced the Lanzhou noodles with hand-pulled noodles that rely on a long resting period to make them extensible. You could also use a dried, thick wheat noodle. But, if you ever get the chance to try the real thing yourself, I urge you, they are truly special.

Add the bones, oxtail and meat into a large stockpot and cover with water. Bring to a rapid boil for 2 minutes. Carefully tip the bones out into a colander and discard the water. Clean the pan. Allow the bones to cool slightly before rinsing and scrubbing them of any dried blood and debris.

Put the meat and bones back into the cleaned pot, along with all the spices and the salt, ginger and spring onion (scallion) whites. Add 4L (140fl oz) of cold water, or enough that the ingredients are completely submerged. Bring to a steady simmer and leave for 3 hours, topping up the pot with more water if the bones or meat become exposed.

If you're making hand-pulled noodles to serve in the broth, now is a great time to make the dough and let it rest before serving (page 32).

After 3 hours, the broth should smell very fragrant and have a glistening layer of fat floating on the surface. Add the daikon and continue cooking for 15 minutes. Scoop out the daikon and set aside.

Remove the beef shin and oxtail from the pot. Strip the meat from the oxtail and slice the beef shin. Set the meat aside for serving and discard the bones.

Strain the soup through a fine mesh sieve (strainer) and discard the solids.

Put a large pan of salted water on to boil.

Cook the noodles according to their instructions on page 35 or on the packet, drain and rinse in plenty of cold water and set aside.

To assemble, season each serving bowl with ⅛ tsp salt, ⅛ tsp MSG, ¼ tsp sugar and 1 tbsp spring onion (scallion) greens. To each bowl, add 300ml (10½fl oz) of hot broth, top with a portion of noodles, the reserved meat and daikon slices. Finish with a red pool of chilli oil on top and coriander (cilantro).

NOTE
Sand ginger (*kaempferia galanga*) is typically translated and labelled as 'dried ginger slices' and comes as lightly coloured knobbly pieces, around the size of a small coin. Liquorice root usually comes whole (looking like straight twigs) or in slices. Both can usually be found in the herbal medicine section of a Chinese supermarket and their aroma and flavour is hard to replicate; so, if you can't find them, leave them out.

Hot Dry Noodles

SERVES 2 · **PREP** 15 MINS · **COOKING** 10 MINS

240g (8½oz) hand-pulled noodle dough
   (page 32) or 100g (3½oz) dried thick
   wheat noodles
200ml (7fl oz) master stock (page 21)
1 pak choi (bok choy) or choi sum,
   leaves separated

To season the bowls
⅛ tsp MSG
¼ tsp Chinese five spice
1 spring onion (scallion), finely sliced
2 tbsp *sui mi ya cai*
1 garlic clove, grated
1–2 tbsp Sichuan chilli oil
2 tbsp *Chinkiang* black rice vinegar
2 tsp toasted sesame oil
2 tbsp Chinese sesame paste
   (loosened with 1 tbsp boiling water)
1 tsp dark soy sauce
1 tsp light (soft) brown sugar

Hot dry noodles, or *re gan mian*, are a staple breakfast dish from Wuhan, in the Hubei province of China. Traditionally they are served with alkali noodles, but I also enjoy the flavours of this dish combined with the chewiness of hand-pulled noodles. Toppings will vary from street vendor to vendor – from preserved radish to crushed peanuts – and I've come to love the addition of blanched greens, although this isn't common either.

Have your hand-pulled noodle dough ready, having rested it for 2–3 hours (page 35). Put a large saucepan of salted water on to boil.

Heat the stock until steaming. Divide all the bowl seasonings between two serving bowls. Pour in the steaming hot stock. Mix well to combine.

Blanch the pak choi (bok choy) or choi sum for 30 seconds, scoop out and set aside. (Keep the water on the pan for your noodles.)

While the sauce sits, follow the instructions on page 35 for pulling the noodles and cooking them. Once floating in the hot water, the noodles should be slippery and silky-looking. Drain the noodles, add these to the sauce in the serving bowls and toss together. If you're using dried noodles, cook them according to the packet instructions and drain, then add to the serving bowls and toss together. Serve with the blanched pak choi.

Glass Noodle Claypot with Prawns

SERVES 2 · **PREP** 40 MINS + SOAKING · **COOKING** 20 MINS

100g (3½oz) mung bean
   vermicelli noodles
1 tbsp Thai light soy sauce
2 tbsp Thai oyster sauce
1 tbsp Thai seasoning sauce
1 tsp Thai black soy sauce
1 tbsp Shaoxing rice wine
1 tbsp light (soft) brown sugar
1 tsp sesame oil
40g (1½oz) coriander (cilantro) root
1 tsp sea salt
3 tsp black peppercorns
2 tbsp neutral oil
½ small onion, finely sliced
2 garlic cloves, finely sliced
2½cm (1in) ginger, grated
6 large, head-on, shell-on tiger
   or king prawns (jumbo shrimp)
100g (3½oz) pork belly, finely sliced
1 tbsp freshly ground black pepper
4 spring onions (scallions), halved

This dish began life with the DNA of the Thai-Chinese dish, *kung op wun sen*. However, with the absence of Chinese celery (I use spring onions/scallions here) and without being cooked over a Thai charcoal grill (called a *tao*), I'm not sure it can be called the same thing. A claypot is essential though – mine is 22cm (8½in) – and you can find them online or in East and Southeast Asian supermarkets.

From my research, I've discovered that kung op wun sen is thought to be Chinese in origin but was adapted with heady aromatics to suit the Thai palate. The aroma of the dish, from the black pepper and fragrant paste, is an important aspect – you smell it before you taste it.

It's important to use Thai soy sauce, oyster sauce and seasoning sauce for this recipe. It will not be the same thing without them – see pages 16–17 for my favourite brands to use.

Place the claypot in a sink and cover entirely with cold water. Let it soak while you prepare the ingredients.

Soak the mung bean vermicelli noodles in boiling water for 25 minutes or until al dente. Once softened, strain and rinse in plenty of cold water. Set aside.

Combine the light soy sauce, oyster sauce, seasoning sauce, black soy sauce, Shaoxing rice wine, light (soft) brown sugar and sesame oil. Pour half the mixture over the noodles and mix to coat.

Slice the coriander (cilantro) root into small pieces and add to a mortar with the salt and black peppercorns. Beat into a coarse paste with a pestle. Alternatively, you can do this in a mini blender. In a heavy-based frying pan (skillet) set over a medium heat, fry the paste in 1 tbsp neutral oil with the onion, garlic and ginger for 3–4 minutes or until fragrant. The onions should retain their shape and texture – you don't want to soften them too much. Remove from the heat and set aside.

Devein the prawns (jumbo shrimp) by cutting along their back shells with kitchen scissors. Fish out the intestinal tract with a toothpick and discard.

Drain the water from the sink and pat the claypot dry. Add the remaining 1 tbsp neutral oil and brush around the bottom of the pot with paper towel or your fingers. Create a single layer of the finely sliced pork belly and add a second layer of the fragrant onion mixture. Pat down with the back of a spoon. Add the prawns in another single layer (this can become a prawny jigsaw but it's important that the prawns are in an even layer to ensure they cook evenly). On top of the prawns, sprinkle a layer of the freshly ground black pepper. Add the dressed noodles, the halved spring onions (scallions) and pour over the remaining half of the reserved sauce. Place the lid on the pot and set over a medium-high heat. Cook for 8 minutes, without lifting the lid! Using an oven glove, carefully remove from the heat and let cool for a few minutes. The prawns should be pink and the bottom of the pot should be crispy.

Tantanmen

SERVES 2 · **PREP** 15 MINS · **COOKING** 15 MINS

For the meat sauce

1 tbsp neutral oil

200g (7oz) minced (ground) beef
   (>15% fat) or 100g (3½oz) each of
   minced (ground) beef and pork

1 tsp Chinese five spice

2 tbsp Shaoxing rice wine

2 tbsp sweet bean sauce or hoisin sauce

½ tsp dark soy sauce

½ tsp freshly ground black pepper

To season the bowls

¼ tsp ground Sichuan peppercorns,
   sieved (strained)

1 tsp toasted sesame seeds

½ tsp light (soft) brown sugar

2 tsp *Chinkiang* black rice vinegar

4 tsp light soy sauce

2 tbsp Chinese sesame paste

2 tbsp Sichuan chilli oil (or to taste)

To serve

2 pak choi (bok choy), leaves separated

200g (7oz) fresh ramen noodles
   (page 40) or 100g (3½oz) dried
   ramen noodles

1 ramen egg (page 19)

600ml (21fl oz) chicken or veg broth
   (pages 20 and 19)

1 spring onion (scallion), finely sliced

Tantanmen **is the Japanese riff on the Sichuanese dish** *dan dan* **noodles. The components are ultimately quite similar, with a few additions and tweaks.**

If you want to make this vegan, simply stick to vegetable broth, replace the minced (ground) meat with soya and leave out the eggs.

Put a large pan of salted water on to boil.

Blanch the pak choi (bok choy) for 30 seconds, scoop out, then set aside. Cook the noodles in the same water until al dente according to the instructions on page 43 or on the packet. Drain, and then rinse in plenty of cold water to stop them from sticking together. Set aside.

To make the sauce, heat the neutral oil in a heavy-based frying pan (skillet) or wok over a high heat. Add the minced (ground) meat and let it caramelize for at least 1 minute, without stirring. Stir, then continue to cook for 5–6 minutes until browned all over. Add the Chinese five spice and cook for 30 seconds. Pour in the rice wine, stir again, then add the sweet bean sauce or hoisin, dark soy sauce and black pepper. Mix well, turn down the heat and cook for another 2 minutes.

Add the ramen egg to a mug of boiling water to gently reheat. Heat the broth until steaming.

To assemble, divide all the bowl seasonings between two serving bowls. Pour in the hot broth and mix well to combine. At the last moment, add the noodles, top with meat sauce, half a ramen egg each, sliced spring onions (scallions) and the blanched pak choi (bok choy).

Curry Coconut Chicken Noodles

SERVES 6 · **PREP** 20 MINS · **COOKING** 40 MINS

1 tbsp coriander seeds

1 tbsp cumin seeds

4–6 dried chillies

2 shallots, peeled

6 garlic cloves, peeled

5cm (2in) ginger, grated

2½cm (1in) *galangal*, finely sliced

1 large or 2 small lemongrass stalks,
   the bottom 5cm (2in) finely sliced,
   the top half discarded

1 tsp mild curry powder

20g (¾oz) coriander (cilantro) root

1 tbsp turmeric root, grated or ½ tbsp
   ground turmeric

1 tsp sea salt

3 tbsp neutral oil

600ml (21fl oz) *chintan* chicken
   broth (page 20)

2 x 400ml (14fl oz) tins full-fat
   coconut milk

3 tbsp fish sauce

2 tbsp Thai thin soy sauce

3 tbsp palm sugar

800g (1lb 12oz) skin-on, bone-in chicken
   drumsticks and thighs, skin on

For the noodles

600g (1lb 5oz) *ba mee* noodles (page 24)
   or 300g (10½oz) dried ramen noodles

500ml (17fl oz) neutral oil

To serve

1 small handful of bean sprouts

1 small handful of coriander (cilantro),
   roughly chopped

3 limes, wedged

2 tbsp chopped pickled jalapeños

2 shallots, finely sliced

2 long red chillies, sliced

This dish is born from a long-time love affair with *khao soi gai* – a northern Thai coconut chicken soup. This paste is reminiscent of a Thai khao soi gai paste, minus shrimp paste and black cardamom, which traditionally give it a distinctive and delicious depth and funk. So, this is my ode to khao soi gai.

The paste can be doubled and frozen into an ice-cube tray, as can the broth, which can be kept in the freezer for a weeknight dinner.

Toast the coriander seeds and cumin seeds in a dry pan until fragrant. Grind with a pestle and mortar, or blitz in a high-speed blender, with the chillies, shallots, garlic, ginger, *galangal*, lemongrass, curry powder, coriander root, turmeric, salt and 1 tbsp of the neutral oil to a fine paste.

Heat the remaining 2 tbsp neutral oil in a heavy-based frying pan. Fry the paste for 3–4 minutes or until fragrant. Add the chicken broth and scrape up any paste that has stuck to the bottom of the pan. Lower the heat, add the coconut milk, fish sauce, soy sauce and palm sugar, and mix well to combine. Simmer gently until the palm sugar has dissolved.

Bring a pot of water to a rolling boil and drop in the drumsticks and thighs. Boil for 3 minutes, then tip the chicken into a colander to drain and rinse with cold water. This removes any impurities and scum. Put the chicken into the coconut soup and simmer on low for 25–30 minutes.

Meanwhile, put a large pan of salted water on to boil. Blanch the bean sprouts for 1 minute, scoop out and set aside. Cook the noodles in the same water until al dente according to the instructions on page 27 or on the packet. Drain, and then rinse in plenty of cold water until they are completely cool – this will prevent them from sticking.

Take two small handfuls of cooked noodles and pat dry with paper towel to remove any water.

Heat the oil in a large saucepan and bring to 180°C (350°F). If you don't have a thermometer, dip the end of a wooden chopstick or wooden spoon into the oil. If bubbles appear, the oil is ready. Drop in one small handful of noodles at a time and cook for 30 seconds–1 minute. The noodles will puff up and turn crispy and golden brown. Remove with a slotted spoon and drain on paper towel. Repeat with the remaining noodles and set aside.

Divide the coconut soup between deep bowls with a portion of soft, blanched noodles and a piece of chicken. Top with the fried noodles, coriander (cilantro), a wedge of lime, chopped pickled jalapeños, sliced shallot, the blanched bean sprouts and sliced red chillies for a kick.

My Ultimate Vegan Ramen

VG · **SERVES** 2 · **PREP** 1 HOUR · **COOKING** 50 MINS

For the broth

1 sweet potato (approx. 300g/10½oz)

1 garlic head

2 tbsp neutral oil

10 baby plum tomatoes (mixed colours), halved

600ml (21fl oz) roasted onion broth (page 19)

2 tbsp hatcho miso or red miso

3 tbsp oat milk

For the nori mushrooms

1 tbsp neutral oil

150g (5½oz) mushrooms (shiitake, oyster, shimeji – one kind or all!)

½ tsp sea salt flakes (kosher salt)

2 tsp light (soft) brown sugar

1 tbsp light soy sauce

½ tsp dark soy sauce

1 tsp sesame oil

1 tbsp ground nori powder or 1 toasted nori sheet, ground into a fine powder

For the crispy chickpeas

neutral oil, for deep frying

1 x 400g (14oz) tinned chickpeas, rinsed with loose skins removed

2 tbsp oat milk

1 tbsp plain (all-purpose) flour

3 tbsp potato starch

4 tsp mild curry powder

½ tsp bicarbonate of soda (baking soda)

1 tsp fine sea salt

To season the bowls

2 tsp chopped pickled jalapeños (with juice)

1 tsp mushroom powder

1 tsp onion powder

2 tsp sesame oil

2 tbsp light soy sauce

This ramen is certainly a labour of love. Don't be put off by the long list of ingredients – all the components can be prepared ahead of time and assembled at the last minute. The broth also freezes really well.

Preheat the oven to 180°C/160°C fan/350°F/gas mark 4.

Toss the sweet potato and garlic head in 1 tbsp of the neutral oil and wrap tightly in tin foil. Set the baby plum tomatoes cut-side up in a baking tin, next to the potato and garlic parcel, and drizzle with the remaining 1 tbsp oil. Bake in the oven for 1 hour or until the sweet potato and garlic cloves are completely soft and the tomatoes are darkly caramelized. Into one bowl, carefully scoop out the sweet potato flesh from its skin (you need 180g/6¼oz in total) and squeeze out the softened garlic cloves from their skins.

Heat the onion broth in a large stockpot and add the miso paste by scraping it through a sieve (strainer) – this will remove any hard lumps. Add the reserved sweet potato and garlic and the oat milk. Using a stick blender, blitz until smooth.

To make the mushrooms, heat the oil in a large heavy-based frying pan (skillet) over a medium heat. Add the mushrooms and salt, making sure the pan isn't overcrowded, otherwise the mushrooms will boil and become slimy. Toss to coat the mushrooms in the oil and leave to brown for 2–3 minutes. Add the light (soft) brown sugar and turn the heat to the lowest setting. Toss the mushrooms once more to coat and let them sit for 5–6 minutes. Don't be tempted to stir or toss them – you're looking for a deeply caramelized colour. Add the light soy, dark soy and sesame oil. Toss to coat, once more, and continue to caramelize over a low heat for 7–8 minutes. Once the mushrooms are darkly caramelized, remove from the heat and sprinkle over the nori powder. Set aside.

To make the chickpeas, pour the neutral oil into a wok or large saucepan to a depth of 5cm (2in) and heat to 150°C/300°F. Drain and dry the chickpeas on paper towel. Combine the oat milk and flour in a mixing bowl, add the chickpeas and toss to coat. In another bowl, combine the potato starch, 1 tsp of the curry powder and the bicarbonate of soda (baking soda). Tip in the chickpeas and toss through with your hands (they will clump together, don't worry).

2 tsp *kombu* powder
2 tbsp mirin
2 tsp light (soft) brown sugar

To serve
200g (7oz) ramen noodles (page 40)
 or 100g (3½oz) dried ramen noodles
200g (7oz) pak choi (bok choy) or choi
 sum, leaves separated
2 spring onions (scallions), finely sliced
2 tsp Sichuan chilli oil (optional)

If you don't have a thermometer, test the temperature of the oil by dropping a small amount of batter into the oil – it should fizzle lightly, not furiously, and bob to the surface when it's ready. Drop the chickpeas into the hot oil one by one and fry in batches (overcrowding the pan will reduce the temperature of the oil, which you don't want) until crisp and golden. Drain on paper towel, season with the salt and the remaining 3 tsp curry powder while they are still hot. Set aside.

Put a large pan of salted water on to boil.

Blanch the pak choi (bok choy) or choi sum for 30 seconds, scoop out, then set aside. Cook the noodles in the same water according to their instructions on page 43 or on the packet. Drain, then rinse in plenty of cold water to stop them from sticking together. Set aside.

To assemble, season each serving bowl with 1 tsp chopped pickled jalapeños (with juice), ½ tsp mushroom powder, ½ tsp onion powder, 1 tsp sesame oil, 1 tbsp light soy sauce, 1 tsp *kombu* powder, 1 tbsp mirin and 1 tsp light (soft) brown sugar. Top with 300ml (10½fl oz) of the hot, enriched broth. Sit the noodles in the middle, and top with the nori mushrooms, roasted tomatoes, blanched pak choi, spring onions (scallions) and crispy chickpeas. Add some Sichuan chilli oil for a splash of red, if you like.

Doubanjiang Aubergine Biang Biang

VG · SERVES 2 · **PREP** 30 MINS · **COOKING** 30 MINS

3 long Chinese aubergines (eggplants)
  or 2 medium aubergines (eggplants),
  sliced into 1cm (½in) batons
2 tbsp fine sea salt
2–4 tbsp cornflour (cornstarch)
  or potato starch
150ml (5fl oz) neutral oil
3 tbsp *Chinkiang* black rice vinegar
1 tbsp light soy sauce
1 tbsp Shaoxing rice wine
1 tsp dark soy sauce
½ tsp sesame oil
1½ tbsp *doubanjiang*
150ml (5fl oz) vegetable stock
  or water (hot)
2 tsp light (soft) brown sugar
1 long red chilli or 2 small red chillies,
  finely sliced
3 garlic cloves, grated
4cm (1½in) ginger, peeled and grated
½ tsp ground Sichuan peppercorns,
  sieved (strained)
360g (12¾oz) biang biang noodle
  dough (page 44)
1 small handful of coriander (cilantro),
  roughly chopped

This signature Sichuanese dish is famously known as 'fish fragrant aubergine' because of its deeply savoury flavour; however, it doesn't actually contain any fish. It's extremely fragrant and spicy from fresh aromatics, including Sichuan peppercorns and *doubanjiang* chilli bean paste. Traditionally it's served with rice but a happy accident in my kitchen proved it works deliciously with slippery biang biang noodles, too.

Place the aubergine (eggplant) batons in a mixing bowl and cover with water. Add the sea salt and mix to dissolve. Use an upturned plate to weigh down the aubergine, so they are completely submerged, and leave for 15 minutes. Drain, then rinse the aubergines and pat dry with a clean dish towel. Dredge the aubergine through the cornflour (cornstarch) or potato starch until evenly coated with a thin layer.

Heat the neutral oil in a wok or heavy-based frying pan (skillet) over a medium-high heat. The oil should be hot enough that when you dip the end of a wooden chopstick or wooden spoon into the oil, bubbles appear. Fry the aubergine in batches – overcrowding the pan will lower the temperature of the oil – for 5–6 minutes or until crispy and golden. Drain on paper towel and allow the oil to cool in the wok.

Combine the *Chinkiang* black rice vinegar, light soy sauce, Shaoxing rice wine, dark soy sauce, sesame oil, and *doubanjiang* with the hot stock or water. Add the sugar and stir to dissolve. Set aside.

Once cooled, remove most of the oil from the wok, leaving around 1 tbsp, and place over a medium-high heat. Once the oil is hot, add the chilli, garlic and ginger and fry for 30 seconds or until fragrant. Add the Sichuan pepper and sauce, stir to combine and bring to a slow simmer. Reduce the heat. Add the aubergine and let this simmer for 2–3 minutes more or until the sauce has thickened. Taste and adjust the seasoning with light soy or sugar, as necessary.

Put a pan of salted water on to boil.

Pull and cook the biang biang noodles according to the instructions on page 47 and transfer straight from the pan into the aubergines and toss to coat. Serve with the coriander (cilantro).

Kimchi & Bacon Udon

SERVES 2 · **PREP** 15 MINS · **COOKING** 15 MINS

50g (1¾oz) thick-cut smoked streaky
  bacon, cut into 1cm (½in) pieces
1 tbsp salted butter
250g (9oz) kimchi (and kimchi juice)
1 tbsp *gochujang*
4 tbsp chicken stock, roasted onion
  broth (page 19) or water
60g (2¼oz) frozen peas
2 tsp freshly ground black pepper
190g (6¾oz) fresh (page 36)
  or frozen udon noodles
2 eggs
1 tbsp neutral oil (optional)
1 toasted nori sheet, finely sliced
1 tbsp toasted sesame seeds
2 spring onions (scallions), finely sliced

During my pregnancy, I really craved spaghetti carbonara. I could eat it night and day and would regularly get out of bed past midnight to rustle it up. I found out later that craving eggs was the body's way of asking for cysteine, an important amino acid for a growing baby.

On one such midnight carbonara quest, I found we were out of spaghetti – and when I spied some udon in the back of the fridge, kimchi also caught my eye.

Serving a raw egg yolk in the middle of the noodles creates such a pretty finish – the yolk will cook from the residual heat of the noodles when tossed through. However, if you prefer, a fried egg is also delicious.

Set a large frying pan over a medium-high heat and add the bacon pieces. Cook and watch the fat render before adding the butter, kimchi, *gochujang* and stock, broth or water. Bring to a gentle simmer before adding the peas. Season with black pepper.

Put a large pan of salted water on to boil.

Cook the noodles according to the instructions on page 39 or on the packet, drain and rinse with plenty of cold water to stop them sticking together. Add to the kimchi sauce and toss to combine. Remove from the heat.

If you're serving with a fried egg, fry these now in the neutral oil. Alternatively, separate the yolks from the whites of the eggs and set aside. Freeze the whites for another recipe.

Serve the noodles topped with nori, sesame seeds, spring onions (scallions), and egg yolk nestled into the centre, or fried egg on top.

Xi'an-style Gun Gun Mian

SERVES 2 · **PREP** 20 MINS · **COOKING** 20 MINS

1 small handful of dried black
   fungus mushrooms
1 small potato, peeled and cubed
1 medium carrot, peeled and sliced
100ml (3½oz) master stock, including
   the fat layer (page 21), or 100ml
   (3½oz) roasted onion broth (page 19)
1 tbsp *doubanjiang*
¼ tsp Chinese five spice
½ small Chinese leaf (napa cabbage),
   chopped into 2½cm (1in) pieces
1 small handful of bean sprouts
240g (8½oz) hand-pulled noodles
   (page 32)

To season the bowls
½ tsp sea salt
½ tsp light (soft) brown sugar
2 tbsp *Chinkiang* black rice vinegar
1 tbsp light soy sauce
¼ tsp ground Sichuan peppercorns,
   sieved (strained)
1 tbsp Sichuan chilli oil or Lao Gan
   Ma Crispy Chilli Oil (or to taste)
½ garlic clove, grated
1 small bunch of coriander (cilantro),
   roughly chopped

NOTE
The noodles served here are called *gun gun mian*, which literally means stick noodles – they are thick and chewy hand-pulled noodles but different from Lanzhou *la mian* in that they do not contain ash (*penghui*) alkali. The extensibility of these noodles relies on a long autolyse process.

This bowl is inspired by the famous Liuxiang noodles, a dish that has been served at Liu Xiang Mian restaurant, in the Bell Tower area of Xi'an, for more than 40 years.

When you enter the restaurant, loud bangs echo from the kitchen, where the expert chefs pull and slap the noodles loudly against the worktop at lightning speed – the slapping temporarily shocks the gluten in the noodle, allowing for extra extensibility. Served with a delicious aromatic gravy, fragrant with Chinese five spice, and packed with beef and vegetables, the dish comes together in under 2 minutes.

On the tables, at the restaurant, you will find chilli oil, vinegar to season and a bowl of raw garlic cloves – the intention is to take a bite of noodles, then a hit of raw garlic.

Soak the black fungus for 15 minutes in boiling water. Strain, then roughly chop the mushrooms.

Put a pan of salted water on to boil. Cook the potato cubes and carrot slices in the boiling water for 7–8 minutes or until al dente.

In a separate pan, bring the master stock or roasted onion broth to a simmer. If using the master broth from chilled or frozen, be sure to include the layer of fat from the top and a good amount of meat. Add the *doubanjiang* and Chinese five spice and stir to combine. Add the Chinese leaf and black fungus mushrooms and let everything simmer gently for 5 minutes or until the cabbage is wilted and the stock has thickened slightly. Add the potato and carrot and continue to simmer for 2–3 minutes. Add the bean sprouts and cook for a further minute. Remove from the heat.

Put another large pan of salted water on to boil.

Pull and cook the noodles according to their instructions on page 35, drain and rinse in plenty of cold water and set aside.

To assemble, season each serving bowl with ¼ tsp salt, ¼ tsp sugar, 1 tbsp *Chinkiang* black rice vinegar, ½ tbsp light soy sauce, ⅛ tsp ground Sichuan pepper, ½ tbsp Sichuan chilli oil (or more, to taste – it's a good idea to taste your broth prior to adding the chilli oil, so you can gauge the spice level), ¼ clove of grated garlic and a small handful of roughly chopped coriander. Divide the Xi'an-style broth between the serving bowls and top with the noodles. Toss well to combine.

Miso Claypot Udon

SERVES 2 · **PREP** 10 MINS · **COOKING** 30 MINS

190g (6¾oz) fresh (page 36)
   or frozen udon noodles
500ml (17fl oz) dashi stock
   (made from powder)
2 tbsp hatcho miso or red miso (see
   note on page 16)
1 tbsp light (soft) brown sugar
2 tbsp mirin
120g (4¼oz) chicken thigh, finely sliced
½ small onion, thickly sliced
3 shiitake mushrooms, rehydrated
   if dried, sliced
4 fried tofu puffs
4 slices of *kamaboko* or
   fried fish balls/crab sticks
1 egg
100g (3½oz) enoki mushrooms
2 spring onions (scallions), thickly sliced
2 *shiso* leaves, folded and finely sliced
½ tsp *furikake* (see note on page 14)

NOTE

Here, I use my Chinese 22cm (8½in)
claypot as used in the Glass Noodle
recipe on page 76 – although a *donabe*
serves the same function, it does look
different.

Nagoya, a city in the Aichi prefecture of Japan, west of Tokyo, is famed for hatcho miso. One of its specialities is *miso nikomi* udon – a hearty warming dish of miso broth cooked and served in a Japanese claypot (*donabe*) with udon noodles and a variety of toppings.

It's really worth seeking out the right ingredients for this dish. You'll find them in East and Southeast Asian supermarkets or online.

Kamaboko is a type of pink *surimi* – aka fish cake – a beautiful topping commonly served in Japan. It has a firm texture and delicate flavour.

Fried tofu puffs add great texture here, while *shiso* leaves (also known as *perilla*), an aromatic herb from the mint family, add a unique and fresh flavour.

Put a large pan of salted water on to boil.

Cook the noodles according to their instructions on page 39 or on the packet (some brands call for microwaving the noodles inside their packaging), drain and rinse in plenty of cold water and set aside.

Add the dashi to a 22cm (8½in) claypot and set over a medium-high heat. Add the miso, sugar and mirin and stir well to combine. Add the chicken and onion slices and bring the pot to a simmer. Cook for 5 minutes or until the chicken turns pale. Add the udon noodles to the broth and arrange the shiitake mushrooms, tofu puffs and *kamaboko* slices on top. Crack the egg into the middle and cook for 2–3 minutes with the lid on. The top of the egg should be cooked but with a runny yolk – if the white hasn't quite set, replace the lid and cook for a further 2 minutes. Add the enoki mushrooms and spring onions (scallions), replace the lid and remove from the heat. To serve, add the sliced *shiso* leaves and sprinkle with *furikake*.

Quick Spicy Seafood Ramen

SERVES 6 · **PREP** 10 MINS · **COOKING** 20 MINS

2L (70fl oz) chicken *chintan* broth
   (page 20)
2 tbsp *gochugaru*
2 tbsp *gochujang*
2 tbsp light soy sauce
2 tbsp oyster sauce
2 tbsp fish sauce
3 tsp light (soft) brown sugar
2 corn-on-the-cob
2 tbsp butter
600g (1lb 5oz) fresh ramen noodles
   (page 40) or 300g (10½oz) dried
   ramen noodles
200g (7oz) Chinese fried prawn balls
6 large tiger or king prawns (jumbo
   shrimp), peeled
300g (10½oz) frozen squid rings or tubes,
   sliced into rings
4 spring onions (scallions), finely chopped
2 toasted nori sheets, quartered

Korean-style broths are my go-to when I want something fast and fiery and this dish is not dissimilar to a Chinese-Korean seafood noodle soup called *jjamppong*.

Having pre-portioned broth, noodles and seafood in the freezer means this dish will come together quickly and easily – making it perfect for a midweek dinner. Typically I make this using dried packet ramen noodles or frozen handmade ramen noodles, if I have them in. If you don't have frozen homemade stock, use a jellied stock cube.

Korean red pepper flakes are known as *gochugaru* and *gochujang* is a Korean fermented red pepper paste. Chinese fried prawn balls are available in the fridge section of East and Southeast Asian supermarkets.

Heat the chicken broth in a saucepan. Add the gochugaru, gochujang, soy sauce, oyster sauce, fish sauce and sugar. Stir well to combine and adjust the seasoning, if necessary. Bring to a gentle simmer.

Brush each corn-on-the-cob with 1 tbsp butter and place under a hot grill. Turn frequently until the corn is cooked and slightly blistered. Allow to cool before standing on its side and running a knife along the cobs to shave off the corn. Some kernels will come off individually, but you're aiming to remove a whole side in one piece. Set aside.

Put a large pan of salted water on to boil.

Cook the noodles according to their instructions on page 43 or on the packet. Scoop out, then rinse in plenty of cold water to stop them sticking together. Set aside. In the same water, cook the fried prawn balls for 4–5 minutes or until cooked through. Drain and set aside.

Devein the prawns by cutting along their back shells with kitchen scissors. Fish out the intestinal tract with a toothpick and discard.

When you're ready to serve, drop the prawns and squid into the hot broth and cook for 1–2 minutes or until the prawns are just pink. Remove the broth from the heat.

Add a portion of noodles to each bowl and top with spicy seafood broth, the corn, spring onions (scallions) and toasted nori.

Spicy Mutton & Tomato Biang Biang Noodles

SERVES 4 · **PREP** 15 MINS · **COOKING** 4 HOURS

5 tbsp neutral oil

600g–800g (1lb 5oz–1lb 12oz) mutton
   or lamb shoulder

1 leek, cleaned and sliced into 3 sections

7 garlic cloves, 5 whole, 2 grated

3 tbsp cumin seeds

3 tbsp fennel seeds

2 tbsp coriander seeds

1 tbsp *doubanjiang*

100ml (3½fl oz) Shaoxing rice wine

4L (140fl oz) water

4 tbsp light soy sauce

3 tbsp light (soft) brown sugar

3 bay leaves

2 star anise

6 large vine-ripened tomatoes, halved

1 tbsp sea salt

720g (1lb 9oz) biang biang noodle
   dough (page 44)

1 small bunch of coriander (cilantro),
   roughly chopped

Sichuan chilli oil, to serve

Biang biang noodles are commonly served with mutton or lamb, both ingredients typically used in Xi'an – the capital of China's Shaanxi province and the eastern hub of the Silk Road – which is testament to the influence the trading route had on local cuisines.

This dish is inspired by a Xi'an-style mutton broth and is laced with cumin and fennel, spices that would have been traded along the Silk Road. Tomatoes are also commonly used; however, they'd usually be added to the broth, or stir fried with eggs. I've slow roasted them here and I love the sweetness they bring.

Heat 4 tbsp of the oil in a large stockpot and brown the meat on all sides. Add the leek, whole garlic cloves, cumin seeds, fennel seeds and coriander seeds, and fry gently for 1 minute. Add the *doubanjiang* and fry for 30 seconds. Add the Shaoxing rice wine and allow the alcohol to bubble away for 1 minute or so. Add the water, light soy sauce, sugar, bay leaves and star anise. Bring to a steady simmer and cook uncovered for 3–4 hours or until the meat is meltingly tender.

Meanwhile, preheat the oven to 110°C/90°C fan/225°F/gas mark ¼.

In a mixing bowl, toss the tomatoes with the grated garlic cloves, remaining 1 tbsp oil and salt. Lay on a baking sheet cut-side up. Place in the oven for 2–3 hours or until the tomatoes are jammy and wrinkly.

When the broth has finished cooking, scoop out the tender mutton and set aside. Strain the broth through a fine mesh sieve (strainer) lined with muslin (cheesecloth), return to the pan and place back over a gentle heat. Shred the mutton shoulder with forks.

Put a large pan of salted boiling water on to boil.

Pull and cook the biang biang noodles according to the instructions on page 47. Drain and serve in bowls topped with shredded mutton, roasted tomatoes and 200ml (7fl oz) strained hot broth. Top with coriander (cilantro) and Sichuan chilli oil, to taste.

Hot Oil Gun Gun Noodles

VG · SERVES 4 **· PREP** 10 MINS **· COOKING** 10 MINS

480g (1lb 1oz) hand-pulled noodles
  (page 32)
2 spring onions (scallions),
  greens finely sliced
4 garlic cloves, grated
4 tsp Sichuan chilli (red pepper)
  flakes or *gochugaru*
4 tsp toasted sesame seeds
6 tbsp neutral oil
3 tbsp light soy sauce
2 tbsp *Chinkiang* black rice vinegar
1 tbsp light (soft) brown sugar

Pouring hot oil over the fresh garlic and chilli powder causes them to sizzle and cook, and results in an instant fragrant dressing for the noodles.

Put a large pan of salted water on to boil.

Pull and cook the noodles according to their instructions on page 35 or on the packet, drain and rinse in plenty of cold water.

To assemble, divide the noodles between the serving bowls and on top of the noodles, in the centre, place 1 tbsp spring onion (scallions) greens, 1 tsp grated garlic, 1 tsp Sichuan chilli (red pepper) flakes or *gochugaru* and 1 tsp toasted sesame seeds. Heat the neutral oil in a small pan, over a high heat, until it's smoking hot. Carefully pour this over the aromatics – it will sizzle and spit, so be careful! Stir to combine. Add the light soy sauce, *Chinkiang* black rice vinegar and light (soft) brown sugar. Stir to combine.

Hotpot

SERVES 4–6 · **PREP** 15 MINS · **COOKING** 15 MINS

FOR THE BROTH

Málà soup

2 tbsp neutral oil

4–5 tbsp *málà* paste (page 18)

3L (105fl oz) chicken *chintan* broth (page 20) or roasted onion broth (page 19)

2 star anise

4 dried red chillies

1 tbsp Sichuan peppercorns

2 bay leaves

5cm (2in) ginger, sliced

6 garlic cloves

Mild soup

1 tbsp goji berries

2 dried shiitake mushrooms

5 spring onions (scallions), halved

5cm (2in) ginger, sliced

3L (105fl oz) chicken *chintan* broth (page 20) or roasted onion broth (page 19)

China, I've learned, is considered the home of hotpot, with a history of more than 1,000 years. Hotpots are now common in many East and Southeast Asian countries in various styles. In Japan, there's *shabu shabu*; in Vietnam you'll find steamboats, Korean hotpot is *jeongol*, and within China there are more than 30 kinds, depending on the region, including Sichuan hotpot, Guangdong seafood hotpot and Beijing mutton hotpot.

The hotpot sits in the middle of the table, consisting of one or two seasoned broths. Accompaniments – proteins, vegetables, noodles, dumplings and dipping sauces – are laid on the table surrounding the pot. Participants dip their chosen bits into the hotpot to cook. Typically, meats and seafood will be dunked into the hotpot first, flavouring the broth as they cook, then secondly, noodles will be cooked in the broth and absorb all the delicious flavours imparted throughout the meal.

To replicate this at home, you'll need a portable heat source, such as a small camping stove and either a Dutch oven, cast-iron casserole dish or a table-top hotpot. And, use any combination of the components listed below to make it your own.

→

FOR THE ACCOMPANIMENTS
(USE SOME, OR ALL)

400g (14oz) fresh ramen noodles (page
  40) or 200g (7oz) dried ramen noodles
400g (14oz) thinly shaved beef (find
  in the freezer section of East and
  Southeast Asian supermarkets)
200g (7oz) Chinese fish balls, prawn balls,
  beef balls
200g (7oz) raw tiger or king prawns
  (jumbo shrimp), peeled and deveined
200g (7oz) squid rings
200g (7oz) fried tofu puffs
200g (7oz) enoki and shimeji mushrooms
250g (9oz) pak choi (bok choy),
  leaves separated
1 small Chinese leaf (napa cabbage),
  chopped into 2½cm (1in) pieces
6–12 dumplings or wontons

FOR THE DIPS
(USE SOME, OR ALL)

Great for meat

1 tbsp light soy sauce
1 tsp sesame oil
1 egg yolk

A good all rounder

1 tbsp *shacha* sauce,
  (see page 133)
2 tsp Chinese sesame paste
1 tbsp light soy sauce
1 tbsp Lao Gan Ma Crispy Chilli Oil
  or similar
1 tbsp chopped coriander (cilantro)

Zingy & fresh

½ a small bunch coriander (cilantro),
  roughly chopped
4 tbsp fish sauce
1 red bird's eye chilli, finely chopped
juice of 1 lime

Simple & classic

1 tbsp *Chinkiang* black rice vinegar
½ tsp sesame oil
1 tbsp light soy sauce
1 tsp ginger, grated

Sweet & spicy

2 tbsp lime juice
2 tbsp palm sugar
2 tbsp light soy sauce
2 garlic cloves, grated
1 red chilli, finely chopped

To prepare the *málà* broth, heat the oil in your chosen hotpot vessel over
a medium heat and fry the *málà* paste until fragrant. Add the chicken or
onion broth and stir to combine. Add the rest of the dried ingredients for
the *málà* soup and bring to a simmer. Turn the heat to low and maintain a
gentle simmer until you're ready to serve.

To prepare the mild broth, add the goji berries, shiitake mushrooms, spring
onions (scallions) and ginger to the hotpot with the chicken or onion broth
and bring to a simmer. Turn the heat to low and maintain a gentle simmer
until you're ready to serve.

To prepare the dips, combine the ingredients listed in small dipping bowls.
For the 'great for meat' dip, the yolk should be cracked into the dipping
bowl and left whole (not mixed).

To serve, set the hotpot over the heat source in the middle of the table.
Arrange the chosen accompaniments on plates surrounding the pot,
along with your chosen dips. Each person will need their own bowl and
chopsticks or serving utensils.

dumplings

Wonton Wrappers

V · **MAKES** 45-50 WRAPPERS

PREP 50 MINS + RESTING

STORE UP TO 5 DAYS IN THE FRIDGE

320g (11¼oz) high-protein flour (11%)
1 tsp fine sea salt
120g (4¼oz) water
3 egg yolks
potato starch or cornflour (cornstarch), for dusting

I am a huge fan of store-bought wonton wrappers – they're thin and this is hard to achieve at home. However, sometimes, the texture and flavour of a homemade wrapper is exactly what's needed. Wonton wrappers differ from regular wheat dumpling wrappers by their thickness and the addition of eggs, making them a lovely shade of yellow.

Add the flour and salt to a mixing bowl and stir through with chopsticks or a fork to separate any large lumps. Whisk the water and egg yolks together, pour into the dry ingredients and quickly combine until a crumbly mixture has formed. Continue to mix until it comes together as a ball of dough. Knead for 1–2 minutes, then turn out onto the worktop. Continue to knead the dough (by hand or in a stand mixer) for 10 minutes or until smooth and elastic.

Mould the dough into a ball and place it inside a freezer bag or in a bowl covered with a damp clean dish towel. Leave to rest at room temperature while you prepare the dumpling filling. If you are preparing the dough more than 1 hour ahead of time, you can leave it to rest in the fridge.

Once rested, take the ball of dough and knead it for 3–5 minutes. Now it should feel very supple and elastic. Using a rolling pin, pressing firmly on the dough, flatten it until it's 5mm (¼in) thick, 15cm (6in) wide.

Set up your pasta roller, clamp it firmly to your worktop.

Pass the dough through the pasta roller on its widest setting. What will emerge might be quite rough and ragged – this is okay! If the dough sheet has separated, or holes have appeared, don't worry. Pass the dough through the pasta roller again on the widest setting and repeat this step until you have one complete sheet of dough, with no holes. Reduce the pasta roller setting to the next thinnest setting and pass the dough through. Reduce the setting once more, to the third thinnest setting. Pass the dough through. Now fold the dough in half, lengthways, and pass through the pasta roller on the widest setting. Repeat this sheeting and folding process until you have a smooth and even-textured sheet of dough. The edges of the sheet may have become dry and cracked – a result of the folding – this is okay. Gently fold the sheet of dough in half and rest at room temperature for 30 minutes, covered with a clean dish towel or clingfilm (plastic wrap).

Once rested, unfold the dough sheet and pass through the pasta roller on the thinnest setting. Dust the entire surface with potato starch or cornflour (cornstarch) and use your hands to coat the sheet of dough. Lay the sheet out on the worktop – you may have to cut the sheet in half so it will fit. With a sharp knife, cut lengthways down the centre of the dough sheet. Using a ruler, cut widthways to create even squares around 7½ x 7½cm (3 x 3in). Sprinkle with a little more potato starch or cornflour before stacking the wrappers, to ensure they don't stick. Wrap in clingfilm or store in an airtight container to make sure they don't dry out.

Dumpling Wrappers

VG · MAKES 25–30 WRAPPERS

PREP 1 HOUR + RESTING

STORE UP TO 24 HOURS
IN THE FRIDGE

340g (12oz) plain (all-purpose) flour
 (11%), plus extra for dusting
1 pinch of fine sea salt
170g (6oz) water

For the dumplings listed in this book, I always prefer making my own wrappers. I love their slight chew and find them much easier to pleat than ready-made. But of course, who doesn't like a quick fix now and again, so store-bought frozen wrappers are perfectly acceptable, too.

Add the flour and salt to a mixing bowl and stir through with chopsticks or a fork to separate any large lumps. Add the water and quickly combine until a crumbly mixture has formed. Continue to mix until it comes together as a ball of dough. Knead for 1–2 minutes, then turn out onto the worktop. Continue to knead the dough (by hand or in a stand mixer) for 10 minute or until smooth and elastic.

Mould the dough into a ball and place it inside a freezer bag or in a bowl covered with a damp clean dish towel. Leave to rest at room temperature while you prepare the dumpling filling. If you are preparing the dough more than 1 hour ahead of time, you can leave it to rest in the fridge.

Once rested, take the ball of dough and knead it for 3–5 minutes. Now it should feel very supple and elastic. Cut the ball into thirds, you will be working with one third at a time, so put the other two thirds back into a freezer bag or covered bowl to prevent the dough from drying out.

Roll the first dough third into a sausage shape, about 25cm (10in) long. You may need to coat your worktop with a sprinkling of flour. Cut the dough into equal 2½cm (1in) pieces. Roll each piece into a ball. If you're not using immediately, store in a container in the fridge.

To make a wrapper, take one of the small dough balls and flatten it, using three fingers, into a small disc, similar to a cookie. Roll the dough as thinly as you can, to form a round, 10cm (4in) in diameter. Make sure there is a light dusting of flour on each wrapper as they are prone to sticking together. Repeat with the remaining dough, working a third at a time to stop the dough from drying out, then prepare in your chosen recipe.

Beef Dumplings in Hot & Sour Broth

MAKES 24–30 DUMPLINGS (TO SERVE 4) · **PREP** 40 MINS · **COOKING** 20 MINS

For the dumplings
500g (1lb 2oz) minced (ground)
    beef (>20% fat)
3 tbsp Shaoxing rice wine
1 tbsp light soy sauce
1 tsp sesame oil
1 tsp fine sea salt
1 tsp light (soft) brown sugar
3 tbsp water
1 tbsp beef dripping or duck fat, melted
½ Chinese leaf (napa cabbage), finely
    shredded
2 spring onions (scallions), finely sliced
5cm (2in) ginger, grated (juice reserved)
4 Chinese leeks, finely sliced
24–30 dumpling wrappers (page 112) or
    450g (1lb) frozen dumpling wrappers

For the vinegar broth
200ml (7fl oz) *Chinkiang* black
    rice vinegar
150ml (5fl oz) water
1 tbsp light (soft) brown sugar
1 piece cassia bark stick
2 bay leaves
2 star anise
1 tsp fennel seeds
1 tbsp Sichuan peppercorns
1 tbsp coriander seeds

To season the bowls
4 tbsp light soy sauce
2 tsp light (soft) brown sugar
4 tsp sesame oil
8 tbsp Sichuan chilli oil or
    Lao Gan Ma Crispy Chilli Oil
1 small bunch of coriander (cilantro),
    roughly chopped
4 tbsp toasted sesame seeds
4 tbsp hot water

One of the most unforgettable things I've ever eaten was in the Muslim quarter of the Northwestern Chinese city of Xi'an, famed for the distinctive cooking of the local Hui community, which is characterized by the use of lamb, beef, cumin and wheat. *Suantang jiaozi* is a dish of juicy and fragrant beef and leek dumplings swimming in a spiced vinegar broth, with chilli oil and coriander (cilantro). It's the sort of perfection that comes from repetition and experience – the skilled chefs at Ma'er Youzhi Suantang Dumplings create more than 100 dumplings per hour and have been serving this dish for more than 30 years. The dumplings are cooked *en masse* in a huge vat – and no matter the time of day, you'll still have to queue for a seat.

I craved this dish a lot when I returned home. The flavour is truly inimitable; this recipe is the result of my experimentation and yearning. A homemade wrapper is preferable here – the thick dumpling is not only deliciously chewy, but the wrapper also ensures the dumpling doesn't go soggy in the broth.

Combine the beef, Shaoxing rice wine, light soy sauce, sesame oil, salt, light (soft) brown sugar, water and fat in a large mixing bowl. Stir with a wooden spoon in a clockwise direction until it resembles a thick, sticky paste – really beat the beef around the bowl to create this texture. You can incorporate a little more water if necessary. Fold in the Chinese leaf (napa cabbage), spring onions (scallions), ginger (and juice) and Chinese leeks until well combined. Put the filling in the fridge while you prepare the broth.

Add the vinegar to a small saucepan with the water, light brown sugar and spices. Set over a gentle heat and warm through until the sugar dissolves. Remove from the heat and allow the broth to sit and infuse, while you prepare the dumplings.

Take a dumpling wrapper in the palm of your hand and place 1 large tsp of filling in the centre. Bring the edges of the wrapper together and gently press the dough to seal the dumpling. You can add some pleats if you want to (see pictures), but this isn't necessary. Repeat with the remaining wrappers and place the completed dumplings on a tray lined with baking paper, at least 1cm (½in) away from each other.

Place the dumplings in a steamer basket lined with baking paper (or a couple of cabbage leaves) at least 1cm (½in) apart. Set the steamer over a pan of boiling water and steam for 8–10 minutes. You may have to do this in batches.

To assemble, season each serving bowl with 1 tbsp light soy sauce, ½ tsp light brown sugar, 1 tsp sesame oil, 2 tbsp (or to taste) Sichuan chilli oil or Lao Gan Ma Crispy Chilli Oil, a small handful of chopped coriander (cilantro) and 1 tbsp toasted sesame seeds. Add the vinegar broth and 4 tbsp hot water. Stir to combine and add the steamed dumplings.

Prawn Wontons with Thai Basil

MAKES 24–30 DUMPLINGS (TO SERVE 4) · **PREP** 30 MINS · **COOKING** 15 MINS

2 tbsp dried shrimp

400g (14oz) tiger or king prawns (jumbo shrimp), peeled and deveined

2½cm (1in) ginger, grated

3 spring onions (scallions), finely sliced

1 tsp sea salt (any kind)

2 tsp light (soft) brown sugar

3 tbsp Shaoxing rice wine

1 tsp sesame oil

¼ tsp ground white pepper

1 tbsp Thai thin soy sauce

1 tbsp fish sauce

1 small handful of coriander (cilantro) stalks, finely sliced

24–30 wonton wrappers (page 108) or 200g (7oz) frozen wonton wrappers

320ml (11fl oz) *chintan* chicken broth

1 small handful of coriander (cilantro) leaves, roughly chopped

To season the bowls

8 tsp *nam prik pao*

4 tbsp fish sauce

1 tsp ground white pepper

2 tsp light (soft) brown sugar

To serve

1 small handful of Thai basil leaves

1 tbsp crispy fried garlic

1 tsp roasted chilli powder (page 18)

Wontons originate in China but are common throughout East and Southeast Asia and beyond. In Thailand, they are commonly served in a clear soup. Here, I have added *nam prik pao* – an ingredient more commonly seen in *tom yum* soup – thanks to a fridge and freezer raid, and it eventually made its way onto my supper club menu.

Toast the dried shrimp in a dry pan for 3–4 minutes or until fragrant. Grind in a mini blender, spice grinder or with a pestle and mortar, to a fine powder.

Place the tiger or king prawns (jumbo shrimp) on a chopping board and mince them by running your sharpest knife through them, scooping them back into a pile in the centre of the chopping board, and running the knife through again. After a couple of minutes, you should have a chunky paste. Add this to a large mixing bowl with the ground dried shrimps, grated ginger, spring onions (scallions), salt, sugar, Shaoxing rice wine, sesame oil, white pepper, Thai thin soy sauce, fish sauce and coriander (cilantro) stalks. Mix well to form a cohesive mixture, and place in the fridge to firm up for 10 minutes.

Take the wonton wrappers and a small cup of water. Begin by adding an even tbsp of filling to the centre of the wonton wrapper. Dip your finger into the water and run this around the edge of the wrapper. Fold the wonton – see the pictures on page 110 for the different ways you can do this – repeat, then arrange the filled wontons on a tray lined with baking paper.

Gently warm the *chintan* chicken broth and put a separate large pan of water on to boil.

Season each serving bowl with 2 tsp nam prik pao, 1 tbsp fish sauce, ¼ tsp ground white pepper, ½ tsp light (soft) brown sugar and 80ml (2½fl oz) hot chicken stock. Stir to combine and dissolve the sugar.

Add the wontons to the pan of boiling water and stir. Cook for 4–5 minutes or until the wontons float to the surface. Scoop out using a slotted spoon, drop into each serving bowl and toss to coat. You will need to do this in batches.

Top each bowl with Thai basil leaves, crispy garlic and roasted chilli powder.

Jalapeño Beef 'Dan Dan' Dumplings

MAKES 24–30 DUMPLINGS (TO SERVE 4) · **PREP** 40 MINS · **COOKING** 25 MINS

400g (14oz) minced (ground) beef
    (>20% fat)
2 garlic cloves, grated
3 spring onions (scallions), finely sliced
2 tbsp chopped pickled jalapeños
1 tbsp jalapeño pickle juice
2 tbsp light soy sauce
1 tsp sea salt (any kind)
2 tsp light (soft) brown sugar
2 tbsp Shaoxing rice wine
1 tsp sesame oil
2 tsp duck fat or beef fat, melted
3 tbsp *sui mi ya cai*
24–30 dumpling wrappers (page 112) or
    450g (1lb) frozen dumpling wrappers
1 tbsp neutral oil

To season the bowls

8 tbsp Chinese sesame paste
2 tbsp boiling water
4–8 tbsp Lao Gan Ma Crispy Chilli Oil
    or similar
4 tbsp jalapeño pickle juice
2 tsp light (soft) brown sugar

To serve

2 tsp toasted sesame seeds
1 small bunch of chives, finely sliced
1 tsp ground Sichuan peppercorns, sieved

I often keep a jar of pre-mixed sauce for *dan dan* noodles in the fridge for a quick weeknight dinner (this recipe is in my first book, *Dumplings and Noodles*) and when I tried it over beef dumplings, it was an instant hit. The combination of the nutty and spicy sauce, with the deep and umami *ya cai* is a match made in heaven.

In a large mixing bowl, combine the beef, garlic, spring onions (scallions), pickled jalapeños and juice, soy sauce, salt, sugar, rice wine, sesame oil and fat. Stir with a wooden spoon in a clockwise direction until it resembles a thick, sticky paste – really beat the beef around the bowl to create this texture. You can incorporate a little more water if necessary. Add the *sui mi ya cai* and stir through. Place the mixture in the fridge while you prepare the dumpling wrappers (page 112).

Take a dumpling wrapper in the palm of your hand and place 1 large tsp of filling in the centre. Bring the edges of the wrapper together and gently press the dough to seal the dumpling. You can add some pleats if you want to (see pictures on page 114), but this isn't necessary. Repeat with the remaining wrappers and place the completed dumplings on a tray lined with baking paper, at least 1cm (½in) away from each other.

Mix the Chinese sesame paste with the boiling water, and stir to dissolve. To each serving bowl, add 2 tbsp of the Chinese sesame paste mixture (this should still be warm from the boiling water), 1–2 tbsp chilli oil (to taste), 1 tbsp pickle juice and ½ tsp sugar. Mix well to combine, until the sugar is dissolved.

Heat the neutral oil in a non-stick frying pan (skillet) over a medium heat, and boil the kettle. Add some dumplings to the pan – they will need at least 1cm (½in) between them, so you may need to cook them in batches. After 3–4 minutes, the bottoms of the dumplings will become brown and crisp.

Add enough boiling water to fill the pan to a depth of about 1cm (½in). This will create a burst of steam, so make sure your face is a safe distance away! Put a lid on the pan and leave the dumplings to steam for 6–8 minutes or until all the water has evaporated. Remove the lid and let the dumplings fry on the bottom of the pan for another minute or two, then remove from the heat and allow to cool slightly – this will loosen them from the pan and make them easier to scoop out.

Serve the dumplings in the sauce, crispy side up. Top with sesame seeds, chives and a pinch of ground Sichuan pepper.

Lamb & Fennel Dumplings with Green Sauce

MAKES 24–30 DUMPLINGS (TO SERVE 4) · **PREP** 30 MINS · **COOKING** 30 MINS

For the vinegar pearls
250ml (9fl oz) neutral oil
100ml (3½fl oz) *Chinkiang* black
   rice vinegar
1 tsp light (soft) brown sugar
½ tsp ground Sichuan peppercorns, sieved
½ tsp agar agar

For the green sauce
80ml (2½fl oz) neutral oil
2 garlic cloves, grated
4 spring onions (scallions), finely sliced
1 green chilli, roughly chopped
2 small handfuls of baby spinach
1 small handful of coriander (cilantro)
   leaves and stems, roughly chopped
1 small handful of coriander (cilantro)
   stems, finely sliced
1 tbsp pickled jalapeño juice
1 tsp sea salt (any kind)
2 tbsp light soy sauce

For the dumplings
2 tsp coriander seeds
2 tbsp fennel seeds
400g (14oz) fatty minced (ground)
   lamb (>20% fat)
2 tbsp Shaoxing rice wine
2 tbsp light soy sauce
2 tsp sesame oil
1 tbsp light (soft) brown sugar
¼ tsp freshly ground black pepper
3 Chinese leeks, finely sliced
6 Chinese leaf (napa cabbage) leaves,
   finely shredded
24–30 dumpling wrappers (page 112) or
   450g (1lb) frozen dumpling wrappers

The spicing of these dumplings is inspired by the cuisines of the Uyghur peoples, a Turkic-speaking Muslim minority whose population is concentrated in the Northwestern Xinjiang region of China. The combination of lamb, cumin and fennel seeds is commonplace, as is the use of wheat, thanks largely to the region's proximity to the historic Silk Road trading route, where these ingredients originally entered China and were traded.

Pour the neutral oil for the vinegar pearls into a glass and place in the freezer for 30 minutes or until completely cold.

Meanwhile, add the *Chinkiang* vinegar to a small saucepan and add the sugar and Sichuan pepper. Heat gently until the sugar is dissolved. Add the agar agar and bring to a boil, then remove from the heat and stir to ensure the agar agar is distributed evenly.

Remove the oil from the freezer. Dip a fork into the vinegar mixture and very gently tilt the fork above the cold oil, to create small droplets. The droplets should fall into the oil to create small spheres. You can also do this using a squeezy dropper bottle, if you have one. Scoop the pearls from the oil and store in a container in the fridge.

To make the sauce, heat the oil in a deep frying pan over a gentle heat. Add the garlic, spring onions (scallions) and green chilli and fry until softened and fragrant. Remove from the heat and add the spinach to the pan. Stir to wilt. Tip the contents of the pan, along with the remaining green sauce ingredients, to a high-speed blender, and whizz until smooth. Chill in the fridge until ready to use.

Toast the coriander and fennel seeds in a dry frying pan (skillet) until fragrant. Grind to a fine powder using a pestle and mortar or spice grinder. Add to a large mixing bowl, with the lamb, rice wine, light soy sauce, sesame oil, sugar and black pepper. Stir with a wooden spoon in a clockwise direction until it resembles a thick, sticky paste – really beat the lamb around the bowl to create this texture. You can incorporate a little more water if necessary. Add the Chinese leek and cabbage and fold through the mix. Chill in the fridge while you prepare the dumpling wrappers.

Take a dumpling wrapper in the palm of your hand and place 1 large tsp of filling in the centre. Bring the edges of the wrapper together and gently

To serve

4 tsp Sichuan chilli oil

2 tsp roasted chilli powder (page 18)

1 small handful of dill fronds

press the dough to seal the dumpling. You can add some pleats if you want to (see pictures), but this isn't necessary. Repeat with the remaining wrappers and place the completed dumplings on a tray lined with baking paper, at least 1cm (½in) away from each other.

Place the dumplings in a steamer basket lined with baking paper (or a couple of cabbage leaves) at least 1cm (½in) apart. Set over a pan of boiling water and steam for 8–10 minutes. You may have to do this in batches.

To each serving bowl, add 4–5 tbsp green sauce and six dumplings. Top with 1 tsp vinegar pearls per bowl and drizzle over Sichuan chilli oil, to create pretty pools of red. Sprinkle with roasted chilli powder and dill fronds.

Crispy Skirt Prawn & Pork Dumplings

MAKES 24-30 DUMPLINGS (TO SERVE 4) · **PREP** 40 MINS · **COOKING** 45 MINS

For the prawn head oil

500g (1lb 2oz) shell-on, head-on tiger
    or king prawns (jumbo shrimp)
150ml (5fl oz) neutral oil
3 garlic cloves
2 lemongrass stalks, bashed
2½cm (1in) ginger, thinly sliced
2 red chillies, roughly chopped
1 tbsp light soy sauce
1 tbsp *gochugaru* or Sichuan chilli
    (red pepper) flakes
1 small pinch of MSG

For the dumplings

200g (7oz) minced (ground) pork
    (>20% fat)
2½cm (1in) ginger, grated
1 tsp sugar (any kind)
1 tbsp light soy sauce
1 tsp sesame oil
1 tbsp Shaoxing rice wine
2 tsp fish sauce
1 tbsp water
½ tsp sea salt (any kind)
1 tbsp dried shrimp, finely chopped
    to a rough powder
2 spring onions (scallions), finely sliced
24-30 dumpling wrappers (page 112) or
    450g (1lb) frozen dumpling wrappers

For the crispy skirt

3 tbsp neutral oil
2 tbsp plain (all-purpose) flour

To season the bowls

4 tsp lime juice
1 small handful of coriander (cilantro),
    roughly chopped

Here, I use the prawn heads and shells to make a rich, deep orange oil to accompany some classic pork and prawn dumplings. The crispy lace on the dumplings creates a delicious web to hold the fragrant oil.

Remove the heads from the prawns (jumbo shrimp) by twisting and pulling the heads away from the bodies, and set aside. Remove the shells by cutting along the back of the shell with some kitchen scissors to reveal the black intestinal tract. Remove this with a toothpick and discard. Peel back the shells and add to the pile of heads. Chop the prawn meat into 1cm (½in) pieces and chill in the fridge.

Add the neutral oil to a small saucepan and set over a medium-high heat. When the oil is hot, add the prawn heads and shells, garlic, lemongrass and ginger. Crush the shells and heads with a potato masher, or the back of a fork, to extract all the juices. Turn the heat to the lowest setting and cook for 30 minutes. Give the shells one last crush before fishing out the garlic cloves. Strain the oil through a fine mesh sieve (strainer) lined with muslin (cheesecloth) or paper towel – be careful, the oil will be hot. Pour in a high-speed blender (or use a stick blender) and blitz the oil, reserved garlic, red chillies, light soy sauce, *gochugaru* or Sichuan chilli (red pepper) flakes and MSG. Set aside.

Beat the pork with the ginger, sugar, soy, sesame oil, Shaoxing rice wine, fish sauce, water, and salt, until it resembles a sticky paste. Fold in the dried shrimp and spring onions (scallions). Place in the fridge until you're ready to assemble the dumplings.

Take a dumpling wrapper in the palm of your hand and place 1 tsp of pork filling in the centre. Sit a piece of prawn meat on top and bring the edges of the wrapper together and gently press the dough to seal the dumpling. You can add some pleats if you want to (see pictures on page 114), but this isn't necessary. Repeat with the remaining wrappers and place the completed dumplings on a tray lined with baking paper, at least 1cm (½in) away from each other.

Heat the neutral oil in a non-stick frying pan (skillet) over a medium heat. Holding a sieve (strainer) about 10–15cm (4–6in) above the pan, sprinkle the plain (all-purpose) flour evenly over the bottom of the pan until there is a thin coating. Add the dumplings in a fan pattern, with about 1cm (½in) between each one. You may need to do this in batches, depending on the size of your pan.

Add boiling water until it fills the pan to about 5mm (¼in). This will create a burst of steam, so make sure your face is a safe distance away! Put a lid on the pan and leave the dumplings to steam for 6–8 minutes or until all the water has evaporated. Remove the lid and let the dumplings fry on the bottom of the pan for another minute or two. A golden brown crust should have formed in between the dumplings. Remove the pan from the heat and let the dumplings cool slightly – this will loosen them from the pan and make them easier to turn out. Place a serving plate over the top of the pan, and invert, to tip the dumplings out onto the plate. Using a butter knife, or your finger, gently crack the crust to separate the dumplings. Each dumpling should be attached to its own shard of crust.

To assemble, divide the prawn head oil between four bowls and add 1 tsp lime juice and a small handful of coriander. Add six dumplings, skirt-side up, to each bowl.

Crispy Skirt Courgette & Black Fungus Dumplings

VG · MAKES 24–30 DUMPLINGS (TO SERVE 4) · **PREP** 35 MINS · **COOKING** 20 MINS

For the dumplings

30g (1oz) dried black fungus mushrooms
200g (7oz) daikon, grated
300g (10½oz or 1 large) courgette
  (zucchini), grated
3 spring onions (scallions), finely sliced
1 tsp sea salt flakes (kosher salt)
1 tsp mushroom powder
½ tsp onion powder
1 tsp light (soft) brown sugar
1 tsp sesame oil
3 tbsp vegetarian stir fry sauce
  (or vegetarian oyster sauce)
1 tbsp light soy sauce
1 tbsp chopped pickled jalapeños
6 tbsp panko breadcrumbs
24–30 dumpling wrappers (page 112) or
  450g (1lb) frozen dumpling wrappers

For the green sauce

80ml (2½fl oz) neutral oil
2 garlic cloves, grated
4 spring onions (scallions), finely sliced
1 green chilli, roughly chopped
2 small handfuls of baby spinach
1 small handful of coriander (cilantro)
  leaves and stems, roughly chopped
1 small handful of coriander (cilantro)
  stems, finely sliced
1 tbsp pickled jalapeño juice
1 tsp sea salt (any kind)
2 tbsp light soy sauce

I came up with this recipe for my vegetarian partner one summer, when our fridge was overflowing with courgettes (zucchini) and greens. Black fungus (or wood ears) are a great store-cupboard ingredient – they add great texture and umami flavour.

Soak the black fungus for 15 minutes in boiling water. Strain, then roughly chop the mushrooms.

Squeeze out the excess moisture from the grated daikon and courgette (zucchini) over the sink. Add the mushrooms to a mixing bowl with the grated veg, along with the spring onions (scallions), salt, mushroom powder, onion powder, light (soft) brown sugar, sesame oil, vegetarian stir fry sauce or oyster sauce, light soy sauce and chopped pickled jalapeños. The mixture will be quite wet at this stage. Add the panko breadcrumbs and mix well to combine. Chill in the fridge to firm up.

To make the sauce, heat the oil in a deep frying pan over a gentle heat. Add the garlic, spring onions (scallions) and green chilli and fry until softened and fragrant. Remove from the heat and add the spinach to the pan. Stir to wilt. Tip the contents of the pan, along with the remaining green sauce ingredients, into a high-speed blender, and whizz until smooth. Chill in the fridge until ready to use.

Take a dumpling wrapper in the palm of your hand and place 1 tbsp of filling in the centre. Bring the edges of the wrapper together and gently press the dough to seal the dumpling. You can add some pleats if you want to (see pictures on page 114), but this isn't necessary. Repeat with the remaining wrappers and place the completed dumplings on a tray lined with baking paper, at least 1cm (½in) away from each other.

Heat the neutral oil in a non-stick frying pan (skillet) over a medium heat. Holding a sieve (strainer) about 10–15cm (4–6in) above the pan, sprinkle the plain (all-purpose) flour evenly over the bottom of the pan until there is a thin coating. Add the dumplings in a fan pattern, with about 1cm (½in) between each one. You may need to do this in batches, depending on the size of your pan.

Add boiling water until it fills the pan to about 5mm (¼in). This might create a burst of steam, so make sure your face is a safe distance away! Gently swirl the pan to distribute the flour. Put a lid on the pan and leave the dumplings to steam for 8–10 minutes or until all the water has evaporated. Remove the lid and let the dumplings fry on the bottom

For the crispy skirt

3 tbsp neutral oil

2 tbsp plain (all-purpose) flour

To serve

1 small handful of chives,
   roughly chopped

4 tbsp Sichuan chilli oil or
   Lao Gan Ma Crispy Chilli Oil

of the pan for a minute or 2. A golden brown crust should have formed in between the dumplings. Remove the pan from the heat and let the dumplings cool slightly – this will loosen them from the pan and make them easier to turn out. Place a serving plate over the top of the pan, and invert, to tip the dumplings out onto the plate. Using a butter knife, or your finger, gently crack the crust to separate the dumplings. Each dumpling should be attached to its own shard of crust.

To assemble, divide the green sauce between four serving bowls. Sprinkle with chives, drizzle with chilli oil and add six dumplings, skirt-side up.

Soy Brown Butter Mushroom Wontons & Crispy Enoki

V · MAKES 24–30 DUMPLINGS (TO SERVE 4) · **PREP** 25 MINS · **COOKING** 35 MINS

For the wontons
25g (1oz) dried porcini (or dried
    mixed mushrooms)
3 tbsp butter
1 tbsp neutral oil
200g (7oz) shiitake mushrooms,
    finely chopped
250g (9oz) chestnut mushrooms
    or field mushrooms, finely chopped
1 tsp sea salt flakes (kosher salt)
1 garlic clove, grated
1 tbsp light soy sauce
2 tbsp vegetarian stir fry sauce
2 tbsp panko breadcrumbs
24–30 wonton wrappers (page 108) or
    200g (7oz) frozen wonton wrappers

For the fried enoki
100g (3½oz) enoki mushrooms
4 tbsp potato starch
200ml (7fl oz) neutral oil

For the soy brown butter
4 tbsp butter
2 tbsp light soy sauce

To serve
1 small handful of chives, finely chopped
1½ tsp freshly ground black pepper

There is something about the nutty, saltiness of brown butter amplified by the umami depth of soy sauce that is simply magic. I could happily eat it off a spoon for three meals a day. Here, though, I've used it to dress mushroom wontons, making them delicious, slick and glossy morsels. This is the kind of dish I would choose to eat alone – revelling in every blissful bite.

Soak the porcini or mixed mushrooms for 15 minutes in boiling water. Strain and reserve the soaking liquor, then finely chop the mushrooms.

In two batches, to avoid overcrowding the pan, add half the butter and oil to a heavy-based frying pan (skillet) and half the shiitake and chestnut mushrooms with a pinch of salt. Cook for 5–6 minutes over a medium heat or until well browned on all sides, then set aside, before repeating with the remaining butter, oil, mushrooms and salt. Return both batches to the pan and add the garlic and chopped porcini or dried mixed mushrooms. Stir and lower the heat to the lowest setting. Cook until the mushrooms are dark and caramelized and the butter smells nutty. Tip into a mixing bowl, add the light soy sauce, vegetarian stir fry sauce and panko breadcrumbs and mix through – this should firm the mixture up a little and soak up any butter.

Take the wonton wrappers and a small cup of water. Add an even tbsp of filling to the centre of a wonton wrapper. Dip your finger into the water and run this around the edge of the wrapper. Fold the wonton – see the pictures on page 110 for the different ways you can do this – repeat, then arrange the wontons on a tray lined with baking paper.

Separate the enoki mushrooms into six pieces and remove the bottom 2cm (¾in) – this bit is usually covered in brown bits – and discard. Flatten the enoki mushroom pieces into a fan shape with your fingers and lay on a baking sheet. Dust well with the potato starch. Heat the oil in a small frying pan to 190°C (375°F) – it should be hot enough that when you dip the end of a wooden chopstick or wooden spoon into the oil, bubbles appear. In batches, add the enoki mushrooms and fry for 1–2 minutes or until just golden. Drain on paper towels.

Heat the 4 tbsp butter in a small saucepan. Once it begins to foam, watch closely, swirling the pan gently, as it will begin to brown and smell nutty. Once browned, add the light soy sauce and 2 tbsp reserved mushroom soaking liquor and stir to combine. Let the mixture bubble and reduce slightly to form a thick glossy sauce. Remove from the heat.

Divide the soy brown butter between four serving bowls.

Bring a large pan of water to the boil and add the wontons. You may need to do this in batches to avoid overcrowding the pan. Cook for 4–5 minutes or until they float to the surface. Scoop out using a slotted spoon and drop six into each serving each bowl. Toss to coat in the brown butter.

Top each bowl with chives, freshly ground black pepper and a fan of fried enoki.

Spicy Prawn & Pumpkin Crystal Dumplings

MAKES 24–30 DUMPLINGS (TO SERVE 4) · **PREP** 45 MINS · **COOKING** 1 HOUR 15 MINS

For the filling

1 small pumpkin or butternut
   squash (roughly 400g/14oz)
1 small red chilli, finely chopped
4 spring onions (scallions),
   finely chopped
1 tbsp miso paste
1cm (½in) ginger, grated
1 tsp fine sea salt
1 tbsp light soy sauce
2 tbsp Lao Gan Ma Crispy Chilli Oil
   or similar
2 tsp sesame oil
35g (1¼oz) Chinese leaf (napa cabbage),
   shredded
4 tbsp panko breadcrumbs
350g (12oz) tiger or king prawns
   (jumbo shrimp), peeled and deveined

For the dumplings

110g (3¾oz) wheat starch
110g (3¾oz) potato starch
200ml (7fl oz) freshly boiled water
3 tbsp lard
neutral oil, for greasing

For the dipping sauce

2 tbsp light soy sauce
2 tbsp *Chinkiang* black rice vinegar

This recipe is an ode to my favourite dumplings at one of my favourite Manchester restaurants, Jade City. Their bright orange pumpkin and seafood dumplings are just heavenly and always appear on my dim sum order when I visit.

To make this recipe vegan, you can switch out the lard in the dough with a neutral oil or vegetable shortening, and omit the prawns altogether, replacing with more pumpkin or squash.

Preheat the oven to 200°C/180°C fan/400°F/gas mark 6.

Pierce the pumpkin or squash with a knife, several times, then place on a baking sheet on the middle shelf of the oven for 1–2 hours or until the flesh is completely soft. Leave to cool slightly.

Scoop out the flesh into a mixing bowl, discarding the skin and seeds. Add the chilli, spring onions (scallions), miso paste, ginger, salt, light soy sauce, crispy chilli oil and sesame oil and mix thoroughly. Fold through the shredded cabbage leaves. Add the panko breadcrumbs and stir. You may need to add more if the mixture is overly wet – the filling should feel firm. If you're making ahead of time, chill in the fridge until you're ready to use.

Chop the prawns (shrimp) in half and set aside.

To make the dumpling dough, combine the starches, add the freshly boiled water and stir to combine. Add the lard and combine well. Once the dough is cool enough to handle, knead it for 10–15 minutes until completely smooth, or mix in a stand mixer with a dough hook for 8 minutes.

Split the dough in half and cover one half with a wet paper towel. Roll the other half into a long sausage, 2½cm (1in) thick. Split into 10g (¼oz) pieces and roll each into a ball. Cover the balls with more wet paper towels. Work with two balls at a time to avoid the dough from drying. Roll the individual balls between your palms until they feel soft and malleable.

Coat the worktop with a small amount of neutral oil. Flatten one of the dough balls with your palm and then roll into a circular dumpling wrapper about 1–2mm (⅟₁₆in) thick and 7–8cm (2¾–3¼in) wide. Add one piece of prawn meat in the centre and top with 1 tsp of pumpkin filling. Gather the edges carefully and seal. Turn the dumpling over, so the pinched side is underneath. Repeat with the remaining dough and filling.

Put a pan of water on to boil.

Cover the bottom of a steamer basket with holey baking paper (you can buy paper like this or simply stab with a skewer or knife to create the holes). Place the dumplings in the steamer basket, make sure they have 1cm (½in) between them. You may have to do this in batches. Steam over the boiling water for 6–8 minutes or until the wrappers are translucent.

Combine the ingredients for the dipping sauce and serve alongside.

Glazed-bottom BBQ Pork & Black Fungus Dumplings

MAKES 24–30 DUMPLINGS (TO SERVE 4–6) · **PREP** 30 MINS · **COOKING** 15 MINS

For the dumplings

1 small handful of dried black
    fungus mushrooms
200g (7oz) minced (ground)
    pork (>20% fat)
1 tsp light (soft) brown sugar
1 tbsp light soy sauce
1 tsp sesame oil
2½cm (1in) ginger, grated
1 tbsp Shaoxing rice wine
2 tbsp *shacha* sauce
2 spring onions (scallions), finely diced
24–30 dumpling wrappers (page 112) or
    450g (1lb) frozen dumpling wrappers
2 tbsp neutral oil

For the glaze

5 tbsp *shacha* sauce
5 tbsp water

To serve

4 tbsp store-bought crispy fried shallots

NOTE

Shacha sauce is a thick sauce made from
garlic, shallots, chillies and dried shrimp.
Its flavour is intensely savoury and umami.
I use Bullhead.

With a crispy and caramelized bottom, this recipe pays tribute to the traditional pot-sticker dumpling technique and those used when making a tarte tatin – only with dumplings and Chinese BBQ sauce (*shacha*).

Soak the black fungus for 15 minutes in boiling water. Strain and reserve the soaking liquor, then roughly chop the mushrooms.

Beat the pork with the light (soft) brown sugar, light soy sauce, sesame oil, ginger, Shaoxing rice wine and 2 tbsp black fungus soaking liquor until it resembles a sticky paste. Fold in the *shacha* sauce, spring onions (scallions) and chopped black fungus, and fold into the mixture. Chill in the fridge until you're ready to assemble the dumplings.

Combine the shacha sauce and water. Set aside.

Take a dumpling wrapper in the palm of your hand and place 1 tsp of pork filling in the centre. Bring the edges of the wrapper together and gently press the dough to seal the dumpling. You can add some pleats if you want to (see pictures on page 114), but this isn't necessary. Repeat with the remaining wrappers and place the completed dumplings on a tray lined with baking paper, at least 1cm (½in) away from each other.

In two batches, heat the neutral oil in a large, non-stick frying pan (skillet) over a medium heat. Add half the dumplings to the pan, 1cm (½in) apart. Add boiling water until it fills the pan to 5mm (¼in). This will create a burst of steam, so make sure your face is a safe distance away! Put a lid on the pan and leave the dumplings to steam for 8–10 minutes or until most of the water has evaporated. Remove the lid and drizzle in half the shacha sauce mixture, until it coats the bottom of the pan. Cook for 2–3 minutes or until it begins to caramelize, then remove the pan from the heat and turn the dumplings out onto a serving plate to reveal their caramelized base. Sprinkle with the crispy fried shallots and serve immediately.

Mapo Tofu Dumplings

MAKES 24-30 DUMPLINGS (TO SERVE 4) · **PREP** 25 MINS · **COOKING** 30 MINS

120g (4¼oz) minced (ground)
  pork (>20% fat)
1 garlic clove, grated
3 spring onions (scallions), finely sliced
1 tbsp *doubanjiang*
1 tbsp Lao Gan Ma Crispy Chilli Oil
  or similar
1 tbsp light (soft) brown sugar
2 tbsp Shaoxing rice wine
1 tsp sesame oil
2 tbsp light soy sauce
1 tbsp chopped pickled jalapeños
1 tbsp pickled jalapeño juice
2 tbsp water
½ tsp ground Sichuan peppercorns,
  sieved (strained)
200g (7oz) firm silken tofu
24-30 dumpling wrappers (page 112) or
  450g (1lb) frozen dumpling wrappers

To season the bowls
4 tbsp Sichuan chilli oil
4 tbsp *Chinkiang* black rice vinegar
4 tbsp light soy sauce
1 small handful of chives, finely sliced
4 tsp chopped pickled jalapeños
  (with juice)

**Mapo tofu is one of my all-time favourite Sichuan dishes – it's
a moreish combination of firm silken tofu and minced (ground) pork
in a rich red sauce. The sauce is a result of the deeply umami and spicy
doubanjiang (fermented broad bean and chilli paste), which carries
the characteristic aromatic and spicy flavours of Sichuanese cuisine.**

Beat the pork with the garlic, spring onions (scallions), doubanjiang, chilli
oil, light (soft) brown sugar, Shaoxing rice wine, sesame oil, light soy sauce,
chopped pickled jalapeños, pickle juice and water, until it resembles a
sticky paste. Fold in the ground Sichuan peppercorns.

Chop the tofu into 5mm (¼in) cubes and fold these into the pork mixture
very gently. They may crumble a little, but you're aiming to have chunks
of tofu running through the mixture.

Take a dumpling wrapper in the palm of your hand and place 1 tsp of pork
filling in the centre. Bring the edges of the wrapper together and gently
press the dough to seal the dumpling. You can add some pleats if you
want to (see pictures on page 114), but this isn't necessary. Repeat with
the remaining filling and wrappers.

Place the dumplings in a steamer basket lined with baking paper
(or a couple of cabbage leaves) at least 1cm (½in) apart. Set over
a pan of boiling water and steam for 8–10 minutes. You may have
to do this in batches.

To assemble, season each serving bowl with 1 tbsp Sichuan chilli oil,
1 tbsp *Chinkiang* black rice vinegar, 1 tbsp light soy sauce, 1 tsp chives,
1 tsp pickled jalapeños and mix to combine. Add six dumplings to each
bowl and toss to coat.

Beef & Ginger Dumplings in Hot Red Oil

MAKES 24–30 DUMPLINGS (TO SERVE 4) · **PREP** 25 MINS · **COOKING** 30 MINS

For the dumplings

400g (14oz) minced (ground)
    beef (>20% fat)
2 tbsp Shaoxing rice wine
2 tbsp light soy sauce
1 tsp sesame oil
1 tsp sea salt (any kind)
2 tsp light (soft) brown sugar
1 tbsp fish sauce
4 tbsp water
2 tsp duck fat or beef fat, melted
4 spring onions (scallions), finely sliced
7½cm (3in) ginger, grated (juice reserved)
2 garlic cloves, grated
24–30 dumpling wrappers (page 112) or
    450g (1lb) frozen dumpling wrappers

For the hot oil

2 spring onions (scallions), finely sliced
3 garlic cloves, grated
3 tbsp Sichuan chilli (red pepper) flakes
    or *gochugaru*
2 tbsp toasted sesame seeds
6 tbsp neutral oil
3 tbsp light soy sauce
2 tbsp oyster sauce
1 tbsp light (soft) brown sugar

These dumplings are inspired by my friend Mei, who runs an independent catering business in my hometown of Manchester, selling her handmade dumplings and family recipe chilli oil (@ohmeidumpling). I always keep a stash of her dumplings in my freezer and her beef and ginger flavour are my absolute favourite. Her recipes are top secret of course, but this is my homage to her, the dumpling queen!

Combine the beef, Shaoxing rice wine, light soy sauce, sesame oil, salt, light (soft) brown sugar, fish sauce, water and fat in a large mixing bowl. Stir with a wooden spoon in a clockwise direction until it resembles a thick, sticky paste – really beat the beef around the bowl to create this texture. You can incorporate a little more water if necessary. Add the spring onions (scallions), ginger (and juice) and garlic, and fold these into the mixture until well combined.

Take a dumpling wrapper in the palm of your hand and place 1 large tsp of filling in the centre. Bring the edges of the wrapper together and gently press the dough to seal the dumpling. You can add some pleats if you want to (see pictures on page 114), but this isn't necessary. Repeat with the remaining filling and wrappers.

Place the dumplings in a steamer basket lined with baking paper (or a couple of cabbage leaves) at least 1cm (½in) apart. Set over a pan of boiling water and steam for 8–10 minutes. You may have to do this in batches.

Add the spring onions (scallions), garlic, Sichuan chilli (red pepper) flakes or *gochugaru* and toasted sesame seeds into a large heatproof bowl. Heat the neutral oil in a pan over a high heat until it's smoking hot. Carefully pour this over the aromatics – it will sizzle and spit, so be careful! Stir to combine. Add the light soy sauce, oyster sauce and sugar. Stir to dissolve. Divide the oil between four serving bowls and add six dumplings to each. Toss to coat.

rice

Oyakodon

SERVES 2 · **PREP** 10 MINS · **COOKING** 20–40 MINS

150ml (5fl oz) *chintan* chicken
   broth (page 20) (optional)
90ml (3fl oz) dashi stock
   (made from powder)
2 tbsp mirin
1 tsp light (soft) brown sugar
4 tbsp light soy sauce
75g (2½oz) chicken thigh,
   sliced into 1cm (½in) strips
50g (1¾oz) chicken breast,
   sliced into 1cm (½in) strips
4 spring onions (scallions), halved
   and sliced into 5cm (2in) pieces
4 medium eggs
300g (10½oz) steamed rice (page 157)

NOTE

For best results, cook each portion
individually – either one after another
or in two pans, side by side.

Purpose-built, long-handled *oyakodon*
pans are typically used for this dish, but
a 20cm (8in) non-stick frying pan (skillet)
works well.

I've learned from my research that *oyakodon* originated at a restaurant
in Tokyo called Tamahide. It was renowned for its chicken *sukiyaki*,
made with its speciality *shamo* chickens – a tall and muscular breed.

In 1891, the fifth-generation owner, Yamada Toku, decided to put the
leftover chicken sukiyaki broth to good use. She added leftover stock
to chicken meat and an egg, and oyakodon was born. Oyakodon, is
the culmination of the words *oyako* meaning 'parent and child' (here
chicken and egg) and 'don' the abbreviation of *donburi* meaning rice
bowl dish.

Tamahide still use home-bred shamo chickens in their recipe. The dish
comes served with a hot cup of shamo chicken broth to start. It is the
definition of comfort.

The simple nature of this dish means the quality of the ingredients
used within it will make a big difference – buy the best chicken and
eggs you can afford. They're the stars of the show, after all. A Japanese
brand of soy sauce is the best option.

For the full at-home experience, serve alongside a bowl of *chintan*
chicken broth. It's not Tamahide, but this version still brings me heaps
of comfort.

Gently warm the *chintan* chicken broth, if using.

Combine 45ml (3 tbsp) dashi, 1 tbsp mirin, ½ tsp sugar and 2 tbsp light
soy sauce in a small non-stick frying pan (skillet) and set over a medium
heat. When the sugar has fully dissolved, the mixture will begin to bubble
and thicken slightly. Add half of the chicken thigh and breast, along with
half of the spring onions (scallions), and spread them evenly around the
pan ensuring some distance between each piece. After 3–4 minutes, the
chicken pieces should almost be cooked through.

Whisk 2 of the eggs and carefully pour over the chicken and seasoning
liquid. Reduce the heat to medium-low and cook for a further 3–4
minutes. At Tamahide, the top of the egg would be served just under-set
and with the perfect wobble. If you prefer your eggs a little more well
done, you can cover the pan with a lid (or a plate) and cook for a further
1–2 minutes. This will thoroughly cook the top of the eggs. Keep the heat
low to ensure the underside doesn't catch and burn.

Serve by sliding the egg and chicken whole over the top of a steaming
bowl of rice. Clean the pan and repeat the process for the second bowl.
Accompany with a bowl of hot chicken broth, if you like.

Chicken Rice

SERVES 4–6 · **PREP** 45 MINS · **COOKING** 1 HOUR

For the chicken
1 whole chicken (approx. 1.8kg/4lb)
  – the best you can afford, I use corn-fed
3 tbsp fine sea salt
7½cm (3in) ginger, sliced
4 spring onions (scallions)

For the rice
3 garlic cloves, peeled and bruised
2½ (1in) ginger, sliced and bruised
1 tbsp neutral oil
450g (1lb) jasmine rice
1 pandan leaf, tied in a knot,
  or 2 bay leaves

For the chilli sauce
7½cm (3in) ginger, grated
4 garlic cloves
4 small red chillies
6 tbsp ground bean sauce
4 tbsp light (soft) brown sugar
1 tbsp dark soy sauce
3 tbsp light soy sauce
3 tbsp *Chinkiang* black rice vinegar
1 pinch of ground white pepper

For the broth
2 ginger slices
2 tsp light (soft) brown sugar
1 tsp fine sea salt
1 pinch of ground white pepper

To serve
1 cucumber, thickly sliced
1 small bunch of coriander (cilantro)
ginger and spring onion sauce (optional)

Commonly known as Hainanese chicken rice, this dish originated in Hainan, China and was popularized all over Southeast Asia, most likely by Chinese migrants, particularly in Malaysia and Singapore. In Thailand you might find it as *khao man gai*, or as *com ga hai nam* in Vietnam.

It may be super-simple in appearance when served, but, as I've learned from experience, each component takes time to perfect and is notoriously tricky to nail. The texture of the chicken, for example, should be juicy but firm, with soft gelatinous skin. Created by poaching and then shocking the chicken, which gives it an almost rubbery appearance, but creates a thin slick of chicken jelly between the skin and the meat. Typically, the meat would be served just cooked and slightly pink at the bone, retaining all of its flavour and juices. The poaching is in turn used to cook the rice and also served as a soup, with a few simple aromatics adding an immense amount of flavour.

This is a dish that requires a bit of trial and error, but with a few handy hints and some attention to detail, this method creates a tasty replica. The chicken, rice and sauce should be eaten together – the broth to soothe the palate and the cucumber to cleanse the palate.

There are many jarred sauces available on the market these days for serving alongside chicken rice – if you can get your hands on a good-quality jar of ginger and spring onion sauce, I would recommend it. In the UK, I'm a massive fan of Sambal Shiok's version, which you can buy online.

Begin by exfoliating the chicken. Yes, really. Rub 2 tbsp of the fine sea salt into the skin of the chicken, on the breasts and legs and into all the crevices. Loose bits of skin and debris should come away from the chicken's skin. Rinse and remove all of the salt. Pat dry using paper towels. The chicken should look shiny, smooth and clean. Remove the neck fat, setting it aside in a shallow dish in the fridge.

Stuff the chicken with the ginger slices and whole spring onions (scallions). Place in a large stockpot and cover with cold water, until the chicken is mostly submerged but the top of the breasts are poking out of the water. Season the water with the remaining 1 tbsp of fine sea salt. Bring to a rapid boil. Remove any scum that floats to the surface and discard. Reduce the heat, place a lid on and cook on a very low simmer for 25 minutes.

Meanwhile, prepare an ice bath big enough for the whole chicken. Carefully remove the chicken from the pot and plunge into the ice water. Don't miss this step. Leave the poaching liquid to cool in the pot.

After 10 minutes, remove the chicken and pat dry with paper towels – it should look rubbery and shiny. Set aside.

In a small blender or using a pestle and mortar, make a rough paste from the garlic and ginger.

Add the reserved chicken neck fat to a large saucepan and set over a medium heat. It will begin to render, and a pool of fat will appear. The remaining fleshy bit of the fat will turn into a little crispy brown blob – remove this. Add the neutral oil to the chicken fat and fry the ginger and garlic paste. Add the rice to the fat and stir to coat. Add 600ml (21fl oz) of the chicken poaching liquid and the pandan or bay leaves. Bring the pan to the boil and reduce the heat. Cover and leave the rice to cook for 20 minutes. Remove from the heat but don't remove the lid for another 10 minutes. Alternatively, transfer the rice, aromatics and stock to a rice cooker and follow the machine instructions.

Meanwhile, add the ginger, garlic and chillies to a mini blender, or using a pestle and mortar, and grind to a fine paste. Add the ground bean sauce, light (soft) brown sugar, dark soy sauce, light soy sauce, *Chinkiang* black rice vinegar and ground white pepper. Taste for seasoning – add another chilli if you want it spicier! Add to a small saucepan over a medium heat and bubble gently for 2–3 minutes or until thickened and lightly caramelized. Remove from the heat and set aside to cool.

Add the ginger slices, brown sugar, white pepper and fine sea salt to the remaining chicken broth and bring to a gentle simmer – it should be clear and have a nice layer of fat. Check the broth for seasoning – add more salt, sugar or white pepper if needed. Strain through a fine mesh sieve (strainer) lined with muslin (cheesecloth).

Strip the dark meat from the bones, and shred with a fork and carve the white meat into 1cm (½in) slices. The skin should stay on the chicken and the meat should be juicy and shiny.

Remove the pandan or bay leaves from the rice.

Serve a portion of rice with some chicken, cucumber slices and a sprig of coriander (cilantro). Serve a bowl of broth and a small dish of chilli sauce alongside. The rice and broth should be hot, the chicken and sauce, room temperature.

Torikatsudon

SERVES 2 · **PREP** 20 MINS · **COOKING** 30 MINS

2 boneless, skinless chicken thighs
60g (2¼oz) plain (all-purpose) flour
¼ tsp fine sea salt
5 eggs
125g (4½oz) panko breadcrumbs
100ml (3½fl oz) neutral oil
125ml (4fl oz) dashi stock
   (made from powder)
2 tsp mirin
2 tbsp light soy sauce
2 tsp light (soft) brown sugar
1 tbsp sake
2 spring onions (scallions),
   sliced into 2½cm (1in) pieces
½ tsp *furikake* (see page 14)
300g (10½oz) steamed rice (page 157)

NOTE

This recipe makes enough for two people using one large frying pan (skillet). If you are preparing this dish for more people, you may need to use more pans or make it in batches.

The same method for this dish is commonly used with pork, too, which is known as *katsudon*.

Torikatsudon **is a delicious chicken and rice dish.** *Katsu* **translates as 'cutlet', which refers to meat that has been bashed into a thin steak, breaded and then shallow fried until crispy.** *Tori* **means chicken – here, breaded and simmered in a sweet, salty, umami broth then topped with beaten eggs and served over steamed jasmine rice;** *donburi*, **meaning rice bowl dish, is abbreviated to 'don'.**

Put the chicken thighs inside a freezer bag or wrap them in clingfilm (plastic wrap). Bash them with a rolling pin until they are about 1½cm (⅝in) thick throughout. Don't bash them too thin – the aim is to get a consistent thickness, so they cook evenly.

Take three shallow bowls or plates. To one bowl, add the flour and salt. To the next bowl, add one of the eggs and whisk. Add the panko breadcrumbs to the third bowl and line them up in this order. Take one chicken thigh and thoroughly coat it in the flour. Dust off the excess and dunk the chicken in the egg, then transfer to the breadcrumbs. Press the breadcrumbs into the chicken to ensure a thick, even coating. Repeat with the second thigh.

Heat the neutral oil in a heavy-based frying (skillet) pan over a medium-heat heat. Drop a single panko breadcrumb into the oil – when the breadcrumb bubbles and rises to the surface, it's ready. Remove the breadcrumb, and carefully add both chicken thighs to the pan using metal tongs. Be careful of hot oil splashing. Fry for 4–6 minutes on either side or until golden and crispy. Remove them from the pan and leave to drain on some paper towels.

To make sure everything is cooked and ready at the same time, the next few steps will need to be coordinated. Clean the katsu frying pan, make up the dashi stock, beat the remaining 4 eggs, and have the other ingredients to hand.

Add the dashi, mirin, light soy sauce, light (soft) brown sugar and sake to the clean frying pan and combine well. Cook over a high heat for 2 minutes or until it starts to bubble. Reduce the heat to medium. Add the spring onions (scallions) to the broth. Simmer until the broth reduces and thickens a little. Add the chicken katsu to the broth and let this simmer for 2 minutes. Pour the beaten eggs over the broth and chicken, to create an even eggy layer.

Reduce the heat to medium-low and cover the pan. Leave for 3–4 minutes – the eggs should be set but still retain a slight glistening wobble and some sauce should remain underneath. If the pan is dry and the eggs firm, it's overcooked! Remove from the heat and serve immediately over steamed rice with a sprinkling of *furikake*.

Gyudon with Japanese Onsen Egg

SERVES 2 · **PREP** 10 MINS · **COOKING** 25 MINS

2 eggs
2 tbsp light soy sauce
1 tbsp sake
1 tbsp light (soft) brown sugar
1 tbsp mirin
1 tsp dashi powder
75ml (2½fl oz) boiled water
1cm (½in) ginger, grated
200g (7oz) skirt/flank/ribeye steak,
  very finely sliced
½ onion, finely sliced

To serve
300g (10½oz) steamed rice (page 157)
1 spring onion (scallion), finely sliced
2 *shiso* leaves, rolled and finely sliced
  (optional), (see page 90)
1 tbsp pink pickled ginger, finely sliced
1 tsp *furikake* (see page 14)

Japanese *gyudon* is finely sliced and braised beef with onions served on top of a steaming bowl of rice. It's a satisfying, fast and reasonably priced meal.

The dish is often served with a raw egg yolk nestled in the middle. I like my gyudon with *onsen tamago*, or 'hot spring egg'. Traditionally, these were cooked in the stable temperature waters of Japanese thermal springs. The sub-boiling temperatures cook the egg very gently, so the white is just set, and the yolk is still runny.

If you buy your meat from a butcher, ask them to slice it as thinly as possible. Alternatively, place your meat in the freezer before slicing with a sharp knife to achieve super-thin slices at home. Thinly sliced frozen beef, intended for hotpot, is available in the freezer section of Chinese supermarkets and also works well.

Place the eggs in a deep bowl and submerge in a larger bowl (or pan) of freshly boiled water. Cover the bowl (with a plate or similar) and let the eggs sit for 15 minutes. Remove the eggs from their water bath and run under cold water to stop the cooking process. Set aside. If you have a thermometer or a sous vide wand, you can be a little more precise – 75°C (167°F) for 13 minutes. Alternatively, this recipe works great with poached or fried eggs, or a raw egg yolk.

Add the soy sauce, sake, light (soft) brown sugar, mirin, dashi powder and water to a heavy-based frying pan (skillet). Bring this to a simmer and let the sugar dissolve. Add the grated ginger and finely sliced beef. Stir to combine and simmer for 3–4 minutes. Add the onions and cook for a further 5 minutes or until the beef is cooked through, the sauce reduced, and the onions cooked but not too soft.

Serve over steamed rice with spring onion (scallion), finely sliced *shiso* (if you have it) and pickled ginger. Gently crack open your onsen egg into a small container – the yolk will be cooked, and the white will be only just set. Plop the egg into the centre of the beef mixture and top with *furikake*.

Miso Chicken Claypot Rice

SERVES 2 · **PREP** 1 HOUR 15 MINS · **COOKING** 20 MINS

1 small handful of dried black fungus
    mushrooms (optional)
240g (8½oz) jasmine rice
240ml (8fl oz) water
2 tbsp light soy sauce
1 tbsp oyster sauce
1 tbsp Shaoxing rice wine
2 tbsp white miso
½ tsp sea salt (any kind)
1 tsp light (soft) brown sugar
1 tsp sesame oil
1 pinch of ground white pepper
2 skin-on, boneless chicken thighs
    (approx. 240g/8½oz), sliced into
    1cm (½in) slices
4 dried shiitake mushrooms, soaked in
    boiling water for 15 minutes, finely sliced
2½cm (1in) ginger, sliced into thin rounds
4 spring onions (scallions), white parts
    kept whole, green parts finely sliced

Claypot rice is the ultimate one-pot meal. There are many styles and variations but all are characterized by the lovely crispy rice you get at the bottom of the pot. Super-comforting and extremely easy to put together, this is my favourite version.

There's something about the smell of the claypot that adds to the comforting qualities of this dish. Claypots are inexpensive and you can find them in East and Southeast Asian markets or online.

Claypots require a gas hob or charcoal flame. If you don't have a claypot, a Dutch oven or cast-iron pot will do. A small rice cooker will also do the trick – layer the rice and toppings as below and set to 'cook'. Just make sure the chicken is cooked through before serving. Or, if you'd like to make this vegan, replace the chicken with five spice firm tofu, and the oyster sauce with vegetarian stir fry sauce.

Place the claypot in a sink and cover entirely with cold water. Let it soak while you prepare the ingredients.

Soak the black fungus for 15 minutes in boiling water. Strain, then roughly chop the mushrooms.

Rinse the rice thoroughly in a sieve (strainer) until the water runs clear. Add to a 22cm (8½in) claypot with the water. Let this soak at room temperature for 1 hour.

Mix the light soy sauce, oyster sauce, Shaoxing rice wine, white miso, salt, light (soft) brown sugar, sesame oil and ground white pepper. Place the chicken thighs in the marinade with the shiitake mushrooms and black fungus (if using).

Nestle the ginger and spring onion (scallion) whites into the rice and water. Layer the chicken thigh and mushroom mixture over the top, including all of the marinade. Don't mix.

Put a lid on the claypot and set it over a medium-high heat and bring to a simmer – steam will begin to escape from the hole in the lid of the claypot. Reduce the heat to low and cook for 12 minutes or until all the moisture has absorbed and the rice is cooked. The bottom of the rice should be nice and crispy. Serve with sliced spring onion (scallion) greens.

Lu Rou Fan

SERVES 4 · **PREP** 10 MINS · **COOKING** 2-3 HOURS

1 tbsp neutral oil
600g (1lb 5oz) skin-on pork belly, diced
    into 1cm (½in) chunks
2-3 garlic cloves, crushed or grated
2 tbsp light (soft) brown sugar
4 tbsp Shaoxing rice wine
1 tbsp runny honey
120ml light soy sauce
1 tsp Chinese five spice
1 small cinnamon stick
1 tbsp dark soy sauce
1 pinch of ground white pepper
700ml (24fl oz) water
6 tbsp store-bought crispy fried shallots
4 medium eggs
600g (1lb 5oz) steamed rice (page 157)

A beloved Taiwanese comfort food, *lu rou fan* is a slow-braised-until-melting meat sauce, served over rice. The texture of the meat varies depending on the region, with chunkier hand-cut pieces of pork belly being more common in the south and mince (ground pork) in the north. Sometimes it is served with hard-boiled eggs.

I first tried this dish in Taipei, served in a paper bowl with a small plastic spoon, and additional condiments on the table. This is my version of that much-loved dish.

In a heavy-based saucepan, heat the neutral oil over a medium–high heat. Add the diced pork and fry until the fat starts to render and the meat begins to turn golden. Add the garlic and fry for 30 seconds or until fragrant. Add the sugar and heat until it starts to caramelize and coat the pork. Add the Shaoxing rice wine and let this bubble gently with the sugar and pork.

Add the honey, light soy sauce, five spice, cinnamon, dark soy sauce, ground white pepper and water, and stir to combine. Bring to a low simmer and stir in the crispy fried shallots. Place a lid on the pan and turn the heat to low. Simmer for 2–3 hours or until the meat is tender and the sauce is thickened and glossy. If the sauce thickens too quickly or begins to burn, add more water (60ml/2fl oz at a time).

Drop the eggs into a pan of boiling water and cook for 5½ minutes. Remove and rinse under cold water to cool before peeling.

5 minutes before serving, add the eggs into the braising meat and toss to coat in the braising liquor.

Serve with steamed rice.

Vegetable Tempura Rice Bowl

V · SERVES 2 · **PREP** 15 MINS · **COOKING** 10 MINS

100g (3½oz) self-raising flour
100g (3½oz) cornflour (cornstarch)
½ tsp light (soft) brown sugar
½ tsp fine sea salt
300ml (10½fl oz) very cold sparkling water
1L (35fl oz) neutral oil
100g (3½oz) sweet potato,
    sliced into 5mm (¼in) slices
4 long-stemmed broccoli
1 small courgette (zucchini), sliced
6–8 oyster mushrooms
2 *shiso* leaves (see page 90)
300g (10½oz) steamed rice (page 157)

For the *tentsuyu* dipping sauce
3 tbsp dashi stock (made from powder)
1 tbsp light soy sauce
2 tsp mirin
½ tsp light (soft) brown sugar
2½cm (1in) daikon, grated

Also known as *ten don*, from the abbreviation of tempura and *donburi* (meaning rice bowl dish), this is a versatile Japanese recipe that is perfect for adapting to seasonal veg. I've listed some of my favourites below.

To keep a super-crispy and non-soggy tempura, it's important to keep the mixture very, very cold. This prevents gluten from developing, and gives a shatteringly crisp finish.

Combine the *tentsuyu* dipping sauce ingredients and set aside.

Sieve the self-raising flour and cornflour (cornstarch) together into a large mixing bowl set on top of a bag of ice or frozen peas, to keep the mixture cold. Add the sugar and salt. Gradually add the cold sparkling water, using chopsticks or a fork to lightly mix – you want to work the mixture as little as possible, to prevent a soggy finish. The finished batter should contain patches of dry unmixed flour.

Heat the oil in a large saucepan or wok and bring to 180°C (350°F). If you drop a small amount of batter into the oil, it should bubble gently, and cook without colouring. If the batter colours quickly or bubbles excitedly, the oil is too hot.

Dip the veg into the batter (keeping the batter sat on the ice or frozen peas to ensure it stays cold) and drop into the hot oil. Do this in batches, to avoid overcrowding the pan, which will cause the temperature of the oil to drop considerably, leading to soggy tempura. Turn once or twice to ensure the veg is thoroughly cooked. The sweet potato should take around 4 minutes, with the rest of the veg taking 2 minutes. *Shiso* leaves should take 30 seconds or so. The batter should only colour very slightly and should remain pale once cooked.

Serve arranged on top of steamed rice with the tentsuyu dipping sauce on the side.

Eggs & Rice Three Ways

Addictive Marinated Spicy Eggs

V · MAKES 6 EGGS (TO SERVE 3) · **PREP** 10 MINS + OVERNIGHT MARINATING
COOKING 6½ MINS · **STORE** UP TO 5 DAYS IN THE FRIDGE (IF YOU DON'T EAT THEM BEFORE!)

6 medium eggs, room temperature
100ml (3½fl oz) light soy sauce
6 tbsp light (soft) brown sugar
100ml (3½fl oz) hot water
4 garlic cloves, grated
4 spring onions (scallions), finely sliced
1 large green chilli, finely diced
1 red bird's eye chilli (spicy) or 1 large
 red chilli (less spicy), finely diced
1 tbsp toasted sesame seeds
2 tsp sesame oil
450g (1lb) steamed rice (page 157)
1 tbsp store-bought crispy shallots

This is a Korean dish that became a viral sensation, and is also known as *mayak gyeran*, which translates to 'addictive eggs'.

Bring a pan of water to a rapid boil. Gently drop the eggs into the water and cook for 6½ minutes. Remove from the water and run under a very cold tap for 3–4 minutes or plunge into an ice bath. When completely cool, peel the eggs.

Combine the light soy sauce with the light (soft) brown sugar and add the hot water. Stir until the sugar is completely dissolved. Add the garlic, spring onions (scallions), green chilli, red chilli, sesame seeds and sesame oil. Add the peeled eggs and cover with a piece of baking paper, so that the eggs are completely submerged. Leave for at least 4 hours, or even better overnight.

Serve the eggs on top of steamed rice, along with 2 tbsp of the marinade, including any bits of garlic, spring onions, chillies and sesame seeds. Garnish with crispy shallots.

Yolk, Rice, Nori

V · SERVES 2 · **PREP** 10 MINS

1 tbsp store-bought crispy fried shallots
1 tbsp *furikake* (see page 14)
1 toasted nori sheet
2 tsp toasted sesame seeds
1 tsp light soy sauce
½ tsp sesame oil
1 tsp mirin
300g (10½oz) steamed rice (page 157)
2 egg yolks

A simple Japanese classic, known as *tamago gohan*, literally meaning 'rice egg', embodies Japanese simplicity in one dish. The hot rice will cook the yolk slightly, turning it pale and thick.

Put the crispy fried shallots, *furikake*, nori and sesame seeds into a mini blender or spice grinder, or use a pestle and mortar, and grind to a rough powder.

Combine the light soy sauce, sesame oil and mirin. Set aside.

Divide the steamed rice between two serving bowls, making a shallow dip in the centre of each. Place an egg yolk into each dip. Spoon over the dressing and sprinkle with the blended nori and furikake powder.

Mix everything together with chopsticks and enjoy.

Crispy Skirt Eggs

V · SERVES 2 · **PREP** 5 MINS · **COOKING** 10½ MINS

2½ tbsp neutral oil
4 spring onions (scallions), shredded
1 tsp Shaoxing rice wine
2 tbsp light soy sauce
2 tsp light (soft) brown sugar
2 eggs
300g (10½oz) steamed rice (page 157)
1 tbsp *furikake* (see page 14)

A fried egg with a runny yolk and shatteringly crispy edge is my favourite way to eat an egg. The trick is to cook it in a traditional carbon steel wok with a round bottom.

Heat ½ tbsp of the neutral oil in a wok over a medium heat and quickly stir fry the spring onions (scallions). Add the Shaoxing rice wine, light soy sauce and light (soft) brown sugar. Bubble away until the spring onions are wilted, and the sauce has caramelized slightly. Pour into a bowl and set aside. Wipe out the wok. Add the remaining 2 tbsp neutral oil and heat over a high heat. When the oil is smoking, crack in an egg. Let it fry until the edges are crispy and brown and the white is just set, the yolk still runny. Remove from the pan to a plate and cook the second egg.

Serve the eggs over steamed rice, with the saucy spring onions.
Top with the *furikake*.

Steamed Rice

VG · SERVES 4–5 · **PREP** 5 MINS · **COOKING** 15–25 MINS

390g (13¾oz) jasmine rice

I always use my rice cooker to prepare rice – I have just never got the knack for cooking to the same standard in a pan – but both methods, using a rice cooker and a saucepan, are included here. The quantities here serve 4–5; simply adjust the amount of rice and water to serve fewer or more people. The basic principle is the same volume of water to rice.

Rinse the rice thoroughly at least three times to get rid of excess starch, then drain.

COOKING IN A RICE COOKER
Place the rinsed rice and 470ml (16½fl oz) of water in the rice cooker and do not stir. Turn the rice cooker to 'high' or 'cook' and leave for 10–20 minutes or until the machine tells you it's done. Leave the lid on for a further 5 minutes. Fluff the rice with a fork and serve.

COOKING IN A SAUCEPAN
Place the rinsed rice and 590ml (20½fl oz) of water in a saucepan and bring to the boil. Reduce the heat to a low simmer, cover with a lid and leave to cook for 15 minutes or until the water has evaporated. Turn the heat off and leave the lid on for a further 10 minutes – don't peek! Fluff the rice with a fork and serve.

sweets

Sichuan Pepper & Orange Ice Cream Wrap

V · SERVES 4–6 · **PREP** 50 MINS + FREEZING · **COOKING** 40 MINS

For the ice cream
560ml (19¼fl oz) double (heavy) cream
450ml (15¾fl oz) full-fat milk
10 large egg yolks
225g (8oz) golden caster
   (superfine) sugar
3 tbsp whole Sichuan peppercorns
2 large oranges, zested and juiced

For the salted peanut powder
200g (7oz) skinless peanuts
200g (7oz) golden caster
   (superfine) sugar
4 tbsp water
15g (½oz) unsalted butter
1 tsp fine sea salt

For the wrappers
125g (4½oz) high-protein flour (11%)
¼ tsp fine sea salt
80ml (2½fl oz) boiling water
135ml (4½fl oz) cold water
1 tbsp neutral oil

To serve
1 small handful of coriander (cilantro),
   leaves picked

This dish is inspired by one I first tried in Raohe night market in Taipei. Three scoops of taro ice cream served inside an impossibly thin wrapper (called *popiah*) and piled high with peanut brittle – shaved with a wood plane from a huge peanut brittle brick. It's the perfect balance of soft, cold, crunchy, chewy and fragrant. The secret ingredient? Fresh coriander (cilantro)!

Preparing popiah wrappers appears to require immense skill, experience, and a little bit of magic. So, I made some tweaks to enable me to make them at home. The final dish, therefore, ended up being slightly different from its inspiration, but it still satisfies my longing, until I can taste it again.

Begin by making the ice cream. Pour the cream and milk into a large saucepan. Bring to just below boiling, then reduce the heat and simmer for 2–3 minutes.

Beat the yolks and sugar together until pale and thickened – I do this in my stand mixer, but you can use a whisk. Gradually pour in the hot cream mixture, with the whisk attachment set to medium-high speed, and beat until well combined. Clean the saucepan and pour the mixture back in.

Place over a low-medium heat and cook for 10–15 minutes, stirring constantly, until just thickened. Make sure to do this over a gentle heat to avoid dreaded scrambled eggs from forming. Once thickened, remove from the heat and pour into a clean bowl.

Toast the Sichuan peppercorns in a dry pan and grind with a pestle and mortar or spice grinder. Sieve through a fine sieve (strainer) into the cream. Stir to combine. Add the zest and juice of both oranges. Leave to cool thoroughly before transferring to an ice-cream machine, following the machine instructions. Once set, transfer the ice cream to a container to be stored in the freezer.

Line a baking sheet with baking paper. Dry roast the peanuts in a dry frying pan (skillet) over a medium heat. They will begin to smell toasty and turn golden brown. Tip onto the baking sheet and allow to cool. In a large saucepan, add the sugar and water and set over a medium–high heat. As the sugar melts and caramelizes, swirl the pot rather than stirring, to ensure it evenly browns. Remove from the heat when the mixture is light golden brown (no darker, as it will continue to colour slightly as it cools) – this should take 10–15 minutes. Add the butter and sea salt and stir to combine. Pour the mixture onto the cooled peanuts, on the lined baking sheet, and tilt to spread evenly. Let it set in the fridge while you make the wrappers.

Mix the flour, salt and boiling water in a stand mixer, or in a large mixing bowl with a whisk. Add the cold water and mix to a silky batter. Using a paper towel, spread a small amount of oil in a non-stick frying pan and bring to a medium heat. Using a pastry brush, brush a thin layer of batter onto the pan, to create a wrapper with a diameter of 15–20cm (6–8in). The batter should start to cook and dry out immediately. Once the top side begins to dry out, flip the wrapper over – there should be golden brown spots on the underside. Transfer the wrapper to a plate and cover with a clean dish towel. Repeat the process with the remaining batter, separating each wrapper with a piece of baking paper, so they don't stick.

Take the chilled peanut brittle and lay another sheet of baking paper on top. Bash it with a rolling pin to break the brittle into smaller pieces, before transferring to a food processor. Blitz until it resembles a coarse powder. Transfer to an airtight jar.

To assemble, take a wrapper and top with two or three scoops of ice cream. Pile high with 3–4 tbsp of peanut brittle powder and five or six coriander (cilantro) leaves. Roll the wrap up, by folding both sides over the filling, and serve immediately.

Fried Bao Buns with Milk Tea Caramel Ice Cream

V · SERVES 8 (WITH ICE CREAM TO SPARE) · **PREP** 45 MINS + FREEZING + PROVING
COOKING 45 MINS

For the ice cream
560ml (19¼fl oz) double (heavy) cream
450ml (15¾fl oz) full-fat milk
4 black tea bags (earl grey works well)
10 large egg yolks
225g (8oz) light (soft) brown sugar

For the caramel
60g (2¼oz) caster (superfine) sugar
¼ tsp fine sea salt
35g (1¼oz) water
3 tbsp double (heavy) cream

For the bao buns
250ml (9fl oz) barista-style oat milk
   (or full-fat milk + 1 tbsp neutral oil)
7g (¼oz) dry yeast
200g (7oz) plain (all-purpose) flour,
   plus extra for dusting
160g (5¾oz) low-protein flour (8%)
   or cake flour
50g (1¾oz) golden caster
   (superfine) sugar
2 tbsp custard powder
½ tsp fine sea salt
1L (35fl oz) neutral oil
3 tbsp golden caster (superfine) sugar,
   to dust

Originating in Taiwan, bubble or *boba* tea – a cold, sweet, tea-based drink with flavoured tapioca pearls – is now a global sensation. I love the flavours of boba and especially as an ice cream, even more so when wedged between doughnut-like fried bao buns.

Of course, if you don't have an ice-cream machine, or simply don't have the inclination, store-bought works just as well.

Begin by making the ice cream. Pour the cream and milk into a large saucepan. Bring to just below boiling, then reduce the heat and simmer for 2–3 minutes. Brew the tea bags in 200ml (7fl oz) boiling water for 4 minutes, then strain. Add the hot tea to the milk mixture.

Beat the yolks and sugar together until pale and thickened – I do this in my stand mixer, but you can use a whisk. Gradually pour in the hot cream mixture, with the whisk attachment set to medium-high speed, and beat until well combined. Clean the saucepan and pour the mixture back in.

Place the pan over a low-medium heat and cook for 10–15 minutes, stirring constantly, until just thickened. Make sure to do this over a gentle heat to avoid dreaded scrambled eggs from forming. Once thickened, remove from the heat and pour into a clean bowl or container. Allow to cool thoroughly before transferring to an ice-cream machine, following the machine instructions. Once set, transfer the ice cream to a container to be stored in the freezer.

To make the caramel, add the sugar, salt and water to a saucepan set over a medium-high heat. The sugar will begin to melt and caramelize. Swirl the pan, rather than stirring, to ensure it caramelizes evenly. Once the caramel is dark amber, remove from the heat and gradually add the cream, stirring constantly. Allow to cool slightly, before transferring to a jug. Let the caramel come to room temperature, and swirl half into the set tea ice cream, using a skewer or a metal knife. Return to the freezer until needed.

To make the buns, warm the oat milk gently in a saucepan for 2 minutes or until warm to the touch, then remove from the heat. If you have a thermometer, make sure the milk is below 50°C (122°F) – if it's hotter, it may deactivate the yeast. If using full-fat milk, add the oil now. Add the dry yeast, stir to combine and then let this sit for 5–10 minutes.

Sift (strain) the flours together in a large mixing bowl, or stand mixer with the dough hook attachment, and add the sugar, custard powder and salt. Add the milk mixture and stir to combine. Turn the dough out onto a lightly floured worktop and knead for 5 minutes or until the dough is even-textured and smooth. Return the dough to a clean bowl and cover with clingfilm (plastic wrap) or a clean, damp dish towel. Place the bowl somewhere warm to prove for 1–2 hours or until doubled in size.

Turn the dough out onto a lightly floured worktop and knead to knock the air out. Roll the dough into a sausage shape and cut into eight–nine pieces (70–75g/2½oz each). Roll each piece of dough into a smooth round ball. The smoother the balls are at this stage, the neater and smoother they will be when they rise. If the dough balls are breaking with cracks forming, let them rest for 2 minutes before trying again. Place the rolled balls on a baking sheet lined with baking paper. Cover with a clean dish towel and leave somewhere warm to prove again for around 30–50 minutes or again doubled in size.

Heat the oil in a wok or saucepan – the oil must be around 5cm (2in) in depth, to ensure the buns float and do not sit on the bottom of the pan. Bring the oil to 180°C (350°F) and reduce the heat to low – if you don't have a thermometer, dip the end of a wooden chopstick or wooden spoon into the oil. If bubbles appear, the oil is ready.

Fry the buns in batches. Transfer them very gently into the oil (a slotted spoon works well here) so they don't lose any air – they should barely bubble. Don't let the oil get too hot and fry them gently for 2 minutes or until golden brown and cooked through. Transfer to a tray lined with paper towels to drain. Sprinkle with golden caster (superfine) sugar while still warm. Leave to cool.

Warm the remaining caramel in the microwave or over a pan of just-simmering water.

To assemble, slice the buns open, stuff with a ball of milk tea caramel ice cream and a drizzle of warmed caramel.

Mango & Coconut Fraisier Cake

SERVES 8–10 · **PREP** 90 MINUTES + CHILLING · **COOKING** 30 MINS

For the genoise sponge

50g (1¾oz) unsalted butter, melted,
   plus 1 tbsp to grease
4 medium eggs
2 egg yolks
125g (4½oz) caster (superfine) sugar
2 lemons, zested
125g (4½oz) self-raising flour

For the crème mousseline

200g (7oz) desiccated coconut
1 vanilla pod (bean), halved
600ml (21fl oz) full-fat milk
4 medium eggs
2 medium egg yolks
180g (6¼oz) caster (superfine) sugar
100g (3½oz) cornflour (cornstarch)
150g (5½oz) unsalted butter, melted

For the mango jelly

350ml (12fl oz) mango juice
   (Rubicon works well)
3 tbsp caster (superfine) sugar
1 tsp lemon juice
1 tbsp dark rum
1 tbsp water
2½ tsp powdered gelatine

To decorate

2 ripe mangoes, peeled and sliced
   into even wedges
150g (5½oz) raspberries
50g (1¾oz) physalis (optional)
edible purple violas (optional)

This French-style cake is based on a recipe by baking doyenne Mary Berry – the original is made with strawberries, lemon and a set custard filling. I first adapted it to make a dessert more fitting for a meal I was serving to Mary herself, during a cookery competition. A bold move, but Mary loved it and I hope you will too!

Preheat the oven to 180°C/160°C fan/350°F/gas mark 4 and grease a 26cm (10½in) springform cake tin (pan) with a tbsp of butter.

Heat a pan of water to just simmering and set a heatproof mixing bowl over it, ensuring the base of the bowl doesn't touch the water.

To make the sponge, add the eggs, egg yolks, sugar and lemon zest to the bowl, and beat until pale, thickened and doubled in volume. When the whisk is lifted through the mixture, any that falls from the whisk should leave a trail on the surface. Remove the pan from the heat and place your bowl on the worktop. Sieve (strain) in half of the self-raising flour and fold through the mixture using a large metal spoon. Add the remaining flour and repeat, ensuring all is incorporated. Be gentle with the mixture to retain as much air as possible. Fold in the melted butter.

Pour the batter into the cake tin and bake for 20–25 minutes or until the edges shrink from the side of the tin slightly and the top is golden brown. Let the sponge cool before turning it out onto a wire rack. Clean the tin – you'll need this later to layer up the cake.

Toast the desiccated coconut in a dry pan over a medium heat for 5–10 minutes, moving the coconut constantly, to avoid burning. Once lightly golden, remove from the heat. Take 2 tbsp and set aside for later.

Tip the remaining toasted coconut into a piece of muslin (cheesecloth), add the vanilla pod (bean) halves and tie the fabric up to create a little infusion bag. Pour the milk into a saucepan, add the muslin bag, and set over a medium heat. Bring the milk to steaming temperature (but do not let it boil) then remove from the heat and let the milk infuse for 20 minutes.

Meanwhile, whisk the eggs, egg yolks, sugar and cornflour (cornstarch) in a large mixing bowl.

Remove the muslin bag from the milk, and pour the infused milk over the egg mixture, whisking constantly. Clean the saucepan and pour the milk and egg mixture back into the pan. Set over a medium heat and stir constantly and furiously for 8–10 minutes, paying particular attention to the bottom of the pan – the mixture will begin to thicken, but keep it moving to avoid scrambled eggs and a lumpy custard. Once thickened, remove from the heat and stir in the butter. Transfer the crème mousseline to a piping bag, balanced in a cup or jug. Chill in the fridge to set.

Add the mango juice to a small saucepan over a gentle heat. Add the sugar, lemon juice and rum, and stir until the sugar has dissolved. Remove from the heat. Mix the water and gelatine together until the gelatine dissolves and add this to the mango juice. Stir well to combine and transfer to a jug. Chill in the fridge for 5–10 minutes.

Remove the base from the cleaned cake tin and place the springform round onto a serving plate. Stand a 10 x 30cm (4 x 12in) piece of baking acetate inside the tin to create an acetate wall around the edge.

Slice through the centre of the sponge, to create two even 3cm (1¼in) thick sponge discs. Place the first inside the baking tin, flattest side down. Line the very edge of the sponge with a piece of mango, then a raspberry, piece of mango, raspberry, all the way around, making sure the fruit pieces are pressed as closely to the acetate as possible, while remaining on top of the sponge. Place some raspberries and mango in the centre.

Take the piping bag of crème mousseline and cut the end off to create a 1cm (½in) hole. Pipe the crème mousseline into the centre of the fruit and then into every crevice you can find. Pipe until all the fruit is concealed – the crème mousseline should be around 4cm (1½in) in depth. Smooth with a palette knife, if you wish.

Place the second half of the sponge on top, with the flattest side facing up. Press gently down and lay 12 thin mango wedges in a clock formation on top of the cake. Pour over the mango jelly. Place the cake in the fridge to set for at least 2 hours or until the jelly is firm.

Sprinkle over the 2 tbsp of reserved toasted coconut and decorate with more raspberries, physalis and purple violas, if using.

Carefully remove the springform edge of the cake tin and carefully peel the acetate away to reveal your masterpiece!

Persimmon Sorbet Baked Alaska

V · SERVES 4 · **PREP** 30 MINS + FREEZING · **COOKING** 45 MINS

For the sorbet

400g (14oz) ripe persimmon flesh,
  skin removed (from around 600g/1lb
  5oz or 4 whole persimmons)
4 tbsp caster (superfine) sugar
2 tbsp liquid glucose
2 tbsp lemon juice
4 tbsp sea buckthorn juice (optional)

For the genoise sponge

4 medium eggs
2 egg yolks
125g (4½oz) caster (superfine) sugar
2 lemons, zested
125g (4½oz) self-raising flour
50g (1¾oz) unsalted butter, melted,
  plus extra for greasing

For the meringue

8 large egg whites
250g (9oz) caster (superfine) sugar

I originally made this sorbet with persimmon and sea buckthorn – the sharp acidity of the latter works really well with the sweet persimmon. Sea buckthorn can be tricky to source, though, so just leave it out if you can't find it. You can also use a store-bought plain sponge here, too.

Preheat the oven to 180°C/160°C fan/350°F/gas mark 4.

Blitz the persimmon flesh in a high-speed blender. Transfer to a saucepan and add the sugar, glucose, lemon juice and sea buckthorn juice, if using. Heat gently until the sugar dissolves, then remove from the heat and allow to cool thoroughly before transferring to an ice-cream machine, following machine instructions, or straight into the freezer in a container for 6 hours.

Heat a pan of water to just simmering and set a heatproof mixing bowl over it, ensuring the base of the bowl doesn't touch the water.

To make the sponge, add the eggs, egg yolks, sugar and lemon zest to the bowl and beat until pale, thickened and doubled in volume. When the whisk is lifted through the mixture, any that falls from the whisk should leave a trail on the surface. Remove the pan from the heat. Sieve (strain) in half of the self-raising flour and fold through the mixture using a large metal spoon. Add the remaining flour and repeat, ensuring all is incorporated. Be gentle with the mixture to retain as much air as possible. Fold in the melted butter.

Pour the batter into an 18–24cm (7–9½in) cake tin (pan) lined with baking paper and bake for 20–25 minutes or until the edges shrink from the side of the tin slightly and the top is golden brown. Let the sponge cool completely before turning it out onto a wire rack. Cut the sponge in half, through its equator, to create two 2cm (¾in) thick discs. Using a 9cm (3½in) cookie cutter, cut out four individual discs.

When the sorbet is set, make the meringue. Add the egg whites and sugar to a clean mixing bowl or stand mixer and beat with an electric whisk for 5 minutes or until the mixture turns to stiff peaks.

When you're ready to assemble, preheat your oven to the hottest setting it will go.

Take each cake round and press a small dent into the centre with the back of a spoon. Place on a baking sheet lined with baking paper. Scoop a ball of sorbet into the centre. Working quickly, pipe or spoon meringue all over the sorbet, so it is completely concealed. Place in the centre of the hot oven for 2 minutes or until the meringue is golden and serve immediately Alternatively, use a blowtorch to cook the meringue.

Miso Chocolate Fondant

V · SERVES 4 · **PREP** 15 MINUTES · **COOKING** 12 MINS

3 tbsp toasted sesame seeds
50g (1¾oz) unsalted butter,
   plus extra for greasing
1½ tbsp white miso
50g (1¾oz) dark chocolate
   (70+% cocoa solids)
1 large egg
1 large egg yolk
60g (2¼oz) golden caster
   (superfine) sugar
50g (1¾oz) plain (all-purpose) flour
150g (5½oz) raspberries

Adding miso to a dessert is a clever and interesting way of adding salt and depth, like salted caramel. And of course, that works perfectly with chocolate.

Preheat the oven to 180°C/160°C fan/350°F/gas mark 4.

Add the sesame seeds to a mini food processor, or using a pestle and mortar, crush to form a coarse powder. Butter four 7cm (2¾in) ramekins or pudding moulds and sprinkle the crushed sesame seeds inside, coating the bottom and edges of the ramekin completely.

Add the butter, miso and chocolate to a heatproof bowl set over a pan of just-simmering water, ensuring the base of the bowl doesn't touch the water. Melt and combine the mix until smooth, then set aside to cool.

Beat the egg, yolk and sugar in a separate bowl until the mixture is thick, pale and airy. Fold in the chocolate miso mixture with a large metal spoon. Sieve (strain) in the flour and fold this through.

Divide the mixture between the four ramekins and place on the middle shelf of the oven to cook for 12 minutes. Remove and leave to cool for 2 minutes. As they cool they should shrink away from the edges of the ramekins slightly.

Carefully invert the fondants onto a serving plate and serve with your favourite ice cream or pouring cream and a small handful of raspberries.

Steamed Custard Buns

V · **MAKES** 10 BUNS · **PREP** 45 MINS + PROVING + COOLING · **COOKING** 30 MINS

For the filling

2 large egg yolks

4 tbsp golden caster (superfine) sugar

100ml (3½fl oz) barista-style oat milk
   (or full-fat milk + ½ tbsp neutral oil)

2 tbsp butter

8 tbsp wheat starch

4 tbsp custard powder

3 tbsp low-protein flour (8%) or cake flour

For the buns

250ml (9fl oz) barista-style oat milk
   (or full-fat milk + 1 tbsp neutral oil)

7g (¼oz) dry yeast

200g (7oz) plain (all-purpose) flour,
   plus extra for dusting

160g (5¾oz) low-protein flour (8%)
   or cake flour

50g (1¾oz) golden caster (superfine)
   sugar

½ tsp fine sea salt

food colouring (optional)

Steamed custard buns are a sweet Cantonese dim sum favourite, called *nai wong bao*. I have fond memories of ordering these from the steaming dim sum trolleys at W H Lung, Liverpool, when I was a child. I began making these in miniature for my daughter at home and experimenting with creating different fun shapes and little animals. These are supposed to resemble little rabbits; however, my daughter thinks they look more like our overweight cat, Marjorie.

To make the filling, set a heatproof mixing bowl over a pan of just-simmering water, ensuring the bottom of the bowl doesn't touch the water. Add the egg yolks, sugar and oat milk (or full-fat milk and oil, if using) and beat until pale and the sugar has dissolved. Add the butter and allow it to melt, and combine. Add the wheat starch, custard powder and flour and whisk to combine. Continue to stir for 6–8 minutes or until the mixture has thickened fully to a thick custard consistency. Cover with clingfilm (plastic wrap) and chill in the fridge (or freezer) to solidify.

To make the buns, warm the milk gently in a saucepan for 2 minutes or until warm to the touch, then remove from the heat. If you have a thermometer, make sure the milk is below 50°C (122°F) – if it's hotter, it may deactivate the yeast. Add the dry yeast, stir and let this sit for 5–10 minutes.

Sift (strain) the flours together in a large mixing bowl, or stand mixer with the dough hook attachment, and add the sugar and salt. Add the milk mixture and stir to combine. Turn the dough out onto a lightly floured worktop and knead for 5 minutes or until the dough is even-textured and smooth. Return the dough to a clean bowl and cover with clingfilm or a clean, damp dish towel. Place the bowl somewhere warm to prove for 1–2 hours or until doubled in size.

Take the filling out of the fridge or freezer, it should be set solid.

Turn the dough out onto a lightly floured work surface and knead to knock the air out. Roll the dough into a sausage shape and cut into ten pieces (60g each). Roll each piece of dough into a smooth round ball. Roll into an oval shape 15 x 10cm (6 x 4in). Scoop 1 heaped dessertspoon of filling into the centre of a dough oval and close by pinching the edges of the dough together to conceal the filling. Gently roll into an oval shape. Pinch each end of the oval into a pointed shape. Using kitchen scissors, snip ears on one end (as shown) being careful not to cut too deep into the dough. Place the buns pinch-side down onto a baking paper lined baking sheet. Cover with a clean dish towel and place in a warm place to prove for a further 30–45 minutes or until puffed up with a smooth dry surface.

Place the buns in a steamer on baking paper squares. They will grow considerably in size, so make sure there is around 2cm (¾in) between each bun. You may need to do this in batches.

Bring a pot of water to a very gentle simmer – if the water is too hot, the buns will blister). Set the basket over the water and steam for 12 minutes. Remove the basket from the heat but leave the lid on for a further 4 minutes. Remove the lid and allow the buns to cool fully, before using a skewer dipped with food colouring to poke eye holes.

Index

Suppliers

The below stock a wide range of East and Southeast Asian ingredients, including store-cupboard, fresh and frozen ingredients, and cookware.

Tuk Tuk Mart | tuktukmart.co.uk
Filipino, Malaysian and Indonesian ingredients

Oriental Mart | orientalmart.co.uk
fresh, frozen and store-cupboard ingredients

Hello Oriental | hello-oriental.co.uk
fresh, frozen and store-cupboard ingredients

Starry Mart | starrymart.co.uk
a wide range of Japanese and Korean ingredients

Sous Chef | souschef.co.uk
a wide range of ingredients

Wing Yip | wingyip.com
a wide range of store-cupboard ingredients

H Mart | hmart.co.uk | hmart.com
fresh, frozen and store-cupboard Korean ingredients

Sushi Sushi | sushisushi.co.uk
a wide range of Japanese ingredients

Japan Centre | japancentre.com
a wide range of Japanese ingredients

Mala Marker | themalamarket.com
for premium Sichuanese ingredients

eFoodDepot | efooddepot.com
a wide range of Japanese and Thai ingredients

Yamibuy | yamibuy.com
great for Japanese, Korean and Chinese ingredients

Acknowledgements

Thank you, with my whole heart, to the amazing team that has worked so hard to bring my second book to life, despite the obstacles thrown our way by the coronavirus pandemic.

Rob, for your effortless styling, for your genuine interest in my recipes, for your dumpling pleating skills, and for your support and being a truly great friend.

India and Magnus, for, like always, capturing my recipes and my processes so beautifully, for making me feel at ease in front of the camera, and for being genuinely ace people.

Han, my Manchester gal, for once again bringing the joy and colour to my work and for continuously going the extra mile. I wouldn't be here without you.

Emily, for translating my vision onto the pages of this book so brilliantly.

Stacey, my editor, for your hard work and patience. For advocating for me and making all of this possible!

Ruth, and the team at Quadrille, for supporting my vision, allowing me so much freedom and for making this possible.

Holly, my manager, for your support, your grounding advice and endless knowledge.

To my circle of Instagram friends – you know who you are – your support has meant everything to me over the last year. I'm so grateful to have you.

To the female business owners that inspire me every day.

Sloth, for having my back, for looking after me and for making me endless cups of tea.

Dad, for supporting me no matter what.

Mum, for lifting me up. For having my back. For being my number one fan.